Likeable

ALSO BY FEARNE COTTON

Bigger Than Us
Little Things

Likeable

HOW I BROKE FREE FROM THE NEED TO PLEASE

FEARNE COTTON

VERMILION/HAPPY PLACE BOOKS

UK | USA | Canada | Ireland | Australia
India | New Zealand | South Africa

Vermilion is part of the Penguin Random House group of companies whose addresses can be found at global.penguinrandomhouse.com

Penguin Random House UK
One Embassy Gardens, 8 Viaduct Gardens,
London SW11 7BW

penguin.co.uk

First published by Vermilion/Happy Place Books in 2026

1

Copyright © Fearne Cotton 2026
The moral right of the author has been asserted.

Penguin Random House values and supports copyright. Copyright fuels creativity, encourages diverse voices, promotes freedom of expression and supports a vibrant culture. Thank you for purchasing an authorised edition of this book and for respecting intellectual property laws by not reproducing, scanning or distributing any part of it by any means without permission. You are supporting authors and enabling Penguin Random House to continue to publish books for everyone. No part of this book may be used or reproduced in any manner for the purpose of training artificial intelligence technologies or systems. In accordance with Article 4(3) of the DSM Directive 2019/790, Penguin Random House expressly reserves this work from the text and data mining exception.

Typeset by Francisca Monteiro

Printed and bound in Great Britain by Clays Ltd, Elcograf S.p.A.

The authorised representative in the EEA is Penguin Random House Ireland, Morrison Chambers, 32 Nassau Street, Dublin D02 YH68.

A CIP catalogue record for this book is available from the British Library

ISBN 9781785046292

Penguin Random House is committed to a sustainable future for our business, our readers and our planet. This book is made from Forest Stewardship Council® certified paper.

To all those who want to give people pleasing the middle finger. To those who have helped me do so.

To Tel, thank you.

I also dedicate this book to myself. For the first time, I'm ready to offer myself the same I offer others.

Contents

Introduction	9
Will You Like Me If … I Behave?	19
Will You Like Me If … I Am Ashamed	37
Will You Like Me If … I'm More Like You?	57
Will You Like Me If … I'm Perfect?	77
Will You Like Me If … I Keep My Mouth Shut?	93
Will You Like Me If … I'm a Big Success?	115
Will You Like Me If … I Tame Myself?	137
Will You Like Me If … I Give You Everything?	157
Will You Like Me If … I Erase My Past?	181
Will You Like Me If … I Don't Age?	201
Will You Like Me If … I Am Small?	219
Will You Like Me If … I Like Myself?	243
Will You Like Me If … I End Things Here?	263
Acknowledgements	267

Introduction

I'm sat opposite my therapist. Let's call her Mary (she's not called Mary). I've had intermittent therapy for years, with varying degrees of success, and have gone through more therapists than King Henry VIII did wives (minus the beheading). But, there's something about Mary (wait, that's a film, Mary is a bad choice of pseudonym. Let's call her Sandra). There's something about Sandra and the space she creates that allows me to peel back many tough layers of skin I have built up over the years to protect myself. Each week, she carefully chips away at this calcified exterior I'm encased in and attempts to communicate with the real me. At this point, I have no idea who that is. I'm so well practised at being 'nice' and palatable that I have completely lost sight of what might be lurking beneath. When my eyes glaze over, Sandra calls me out: 'Fearne, where have you gone?' I'm well versed in always doing the *right* thing, and at times this means disassociating with what's going on around me so that I don't have a sudden burst of emotion.

Sandra discusses a subject I'm finding difficult to stomach and I can feel my brain slowly blurring. The hard lines of reality soften into a pixelated haze that lacks the necessary force to impact me. A pleasant smile is plastered on my face

INTRODUCTION

to disguise the inner distress I'm suppressing, but she can see it in my eyes. Dead, blank, without any signs of life. 'Hello, Fearne, are you in there?' Good question. I have no idea.

But today she breaks me. I have been coming to see Sandra weekly for around eight months and have only politely wept tears on one occasion after a friend of mine died. Sadness and anger feel too deeply buried to reach. I have an inkling that rage is bubbling internally and that a dam is holding back years' worth of tears, but I'm only allowing myself to skim the surface of the feelings present. Yet, on this grey Wednesday, sat in Sandra's front room, I'm caught off-guard.

'How important is it that I like you?' she asks softly.

First, my chest starts to heave. Undulating waves of physical spasm rise from my solar plexus like a tsunami of trapped pain. My mouth opens but only wisps of stuttered air come out.

'What's going on?' she asks with even more care and gentleness, her voice a soft hug from across the room.

There aren't any words that can describe what I'm feeling – or, perhaps more accurately, what I'm not allowing myself to feel. The tears start and won't stop. A door has been unlocked but I'm unsure of what's behind it. Why has this one question hit so deeply? Why do I care if Sandra likes me or not? Clearly, I care a lot.

Hours after the session, I am still asking myself these same questions. Why do I so desperately want her to like me? I'm paying her to be my therapist. She isn't a friend, nor

INTRODUCTION

somebody I'm likely to get to know outside of a therapeutic setting. I'm there to get to the bottom of some of my darkest thoughts and shadows lurking in the past, not to make a new friend. So why am I so hell-bent on her liking me? And why did that one question – 'How important is it that I like you?' – crack me in two?

What does it even mean to be likeable? For some of us, it might mean keeping the peace. Constant shape-shifting to mitigate as much chaos and stress as possible. For others, it might mean getting praise and recognition for our efforts and good nature. For each of us, it'll look and feel different because it's such a complex concept. On the surface, being likeable may seem like a positive quality. You are a good egg, a decent human, with values and a nurturing personality. This may well be true, but the problems come when being likeable means placating others by repressing our own true wants and desires – at worst, even burying whole parts of ourselves that we deem 'unlikeable' just to fit in or head off any pushback or rejection. For many of us, consciously or unconsciously, it becomes a weapon we use to self-flagellate and torture ourselves when we feel we have failed or upset someone. We want to be the *good girl* at all costs – and there is always a cost.

Wanting to be liked by others leads to people pleasing, and if we are people pleasing, then we are most definitely suppressing

INTRODUCTION

feelings, words, actions and desires. And there's only so much shoving and concealing we are capable of before it all starts to spill over into every corner of life. We may even ask ourselves: if we do not feel liked by everyone else, are we still allowed to like ourselves? That last question is one I've spent years pondering.

Through my therapy sessions with Sandra, I was starting to get a sense of how much was buried in my basement. Bin bags of resentment, sacks of rage, a skip full of unspoken words and whole parts of my personality covered in the tar of other people's comments and opinions. The price of keeping this shit buried but wrapped in a pretty, pink, aesthetically pleasing bow so no one can see it has been huge for me: insomnia, OCD, bulimia, panic attacks and, more recently, a trip to hospital for an unexpected operation. We'll get to that later. It might read like a grim list, but I have an inkling that you have one of your own. The flavour might differ, the severity may vary, but you'll have an itemised bill of what people pleasing has cost you too.

I also came to realise that people pleasing makes me so tired. A low-level exhaustion that I wear like a heavy winter coat. It's wrapped around each limb and pulls me closer to the ground, yet never entirely halts me. I keep going. I have to. We have to. We have jobs to succeed in, school snack boxes to fill, bills to pay, friends to keep up with, partners to attend to, exercise routines to continue, ideals to actualise. *We must never stop*, we tell ourselves. Plus, staying busy keeps us from

INTRODUCTION

looking at our true desires: the things we secretly really want, the life we desperately wish for. If we keep distracting ourselves, we don't have the time or space to really look at what we desire and won't have to change our people-pleasing ways.

Staying likeable, a good little people pleaser, seems easier in the moment. It's surely less of a hassle to trudge on in the same too-tight, people-pleasing shoes; we are used to it. We know what will please others and we therefore know how they will react. So, of course, we stay preoccupied. If we give ourselves more time and space, we will also allow ourselves the mental clarity to see what we want. TERRIFYING. Because when we know what we want, we have to make changes. And those changes might not please others, might just rock the boat, and, at worst, might make us utterly unlikeable. Women have been told there are certain rules we must abide by if we want to be likeable, be approved of, pass the test. The way we look, act, lead, speak and express ourselves is scrutinised in a way that leaves us feeling claustrophobic.

Be good, do as you're told, work hard, never pause, be clever, always say the right thing, be polite, don't say no, always show up, look pretty, be small, don't swear, say nice things, don't have an opinion, don't be too loud, don't be too quiet, eat well – but not too much, look great, don't look too great, be feminine, don't be slutty, be perfect, but don't be *too* successful, reach life's milestones, don't boast, don't be weird, don't give up, don't walk away, smile – and then maybe, just maybe, you'll be likeable.

INTRODUCTION

We all know the rules. We have internalised them, starting from when we were tiny. And yet, a lot of the time, we have no clue we are censoring ourselves or keeping our minds from our true desires. We are so used to placating, agreeing, supporting that we forget to ask ourselves what we want and how we want to show up in the world. Our autonomous minds converge with outside opinion, societal pressures and stereotypes to the point where we lose our innate sense of what is right for us as individuals.

Do you want kids, or have you been told you're supposed to want them? Do you want to climb the ladder at work, or do you feel outside pressure to prove yourself? Do you want to hang out with that person, or have you been convinced it's terribly selfish to walk away? For us to make decisions from a true, deep, burning place of desire feels reckless and could lead to, I don't know, some kind of revolution.

So why are we not charging towards a revolution? Personally, I'm only just starting to charge (maybe a light trot) towards great change because I've been previously wracked with the fear of outside opinion. Its only now, in my forties, that I'm questioning how much of it I need to listen to. Do you feel the same? The judgement we feel might come from those around us, but it also trickles steadily down from years of patriarchal indoctrination.

Bloody hell, I have fire in my belly as I type these words. Unruly, unconfined, unpalatable fire. I've realised writing about this subject brings up deep rumblings of frustration that

INTRODUCTION

seem to predate my little life. As if each woman that's come before me who has kept her true self and desires buried deep to please others is waving a fist in the air, demanding change. I feel irritated that so many of us have been indoctrinated to believe we have to hide parts of ourselves to be likeable. We've diluted and reduced ourselves to simply be liked.

I feel pissed off that I've morphed into a version of myself other people have needed me to be, taken on too much responsibility, put myself down, shrunk and stayed quiet – all in the hope I would be liked. I can look back on whole chunks of my life and see how unsure I felt about myself. I either didn't feel enough, and so supercharged my personality in a desperate attempt to be seen as funny and vibrant, or I was so fearful that every word that came out of my mouth was wrong that I stayed silent.

This judgement that's held over our heads has sadly also seeped into how we view each other: women slagging off other women without really understanding why. We've been brainwashed to judge other women rather than liberate ourselves. Because of course when we are trapped and see a woman who has freed herself to recognise her own desires, we judge her rather than look to her for inspiration. We are encouraged to deem anyone who steps outside of the lines unlikeable rather than intriguing. I've fallen into this trap many a time myself. Someone breaks the rules and rather than be inquisitive, I get my pointy finger out and wag it.

I'm angry that I have done that and I am angry about the

INTRODUCTION

reasons for it. Anger can be debilitating if not dealt with properly, but when used to fuel passion and to combat fear, it can lead to immense change. That's what I'm hoping for. Great change for me and for you too. But of course, we aren't meant to be angry. That would make us highly unlikeable.

What I want us to do here is not just ask why so many of us are obsessively worried about being liked, but also to ponder how we can change that mindset and subsequently get cosy in the discomfort of being, dare I say it, disliked.

How does that feel, even to say out loud? *Disliked*. Ouch. It hurts, and I think I know why – but we will get to all of this in good time.

We also need to dive headfirst into why we have become so culturally fixated on being likeable, and how its dirty little promise of self-worth and freedom is actually hiding a much darker secret – that it is in fact the set of handcuffs for a life sentence of feeling muted and unfulfilled.

What made me want to write about this murky, uncomfortable subject? Why am I lifting this particular rock that we are expected to leave well alone? And, hell, why should you even listen to me?

I'm the first to admit I'm not an expert on anything. I know a lot about music, but I'm not an expert. I know a lot about wellbeing, but I'm not an expert. Yet I believe I am an expert when it comes to being likeable. You see, I've worked in a job where being likeable is everything. Since the age of fifteen, I've mastered how to appear likeable to others. I have

INTRODUCTION

LOVED my job and been fortunate that it has allowed me to do some amazing things and meet some incredible people. However, the reality of it meant that from my mid teens, I was made aware that there were future opportunities, money and public opinion resting on how likeable I was able to make myself. Being disliked by a couple of girls at school felt no heavier than a benign irritation, whereas strangers with an opinion watching you on TV felt like personality annihilation. Yet the real weight of that didn't properly hit me until much later down the line.

You could even say that I am actually overqualified in this field, as I have had brief encounters with being publicly very unliked. So, I've very much seen and felt both sides of the coin. Like you, there are also a handful of people out there who do know me (not just from the telly) and do not like me. Always a queasy and unnerving sensation, but not impossible to live alongside. We'll get to this down the line too.

We've got centuries of toxic messaging to wade through, years of our own personal conditioning to excavate and many a myth to dispel, so let's get on with it. Will you like me if I write a polite little book that won't feel at times confronting, and won't challenge your beliefs? Maybe, but that's not what this is. At last, I'm not here to be liked.

Will You Like Me If ... I Behave?

I'm sixteen and have just had my braces removed. My teeth feel extra smooth and too big for my mouth; my tongue constantly runs back and forth over the surface in delight. I'm sat in a treehouse in a white T-shirt and jeans with an aching smile plastered on my face. I must keep smiling. I'm happy, that's certain, but the smile has to stay in place to show that I understand what is expected of me.

People move around, adjusting microphones, wafting booms overhead and talking at pace into headsets. I run my lines in my head again whilst trying to block out the distractions all around. Exhilaration pulses through my every cell. I've done it. I've made it onto the TV. Hours of daydreaming of this moment whilst in maths class, years of dance and drama lessons at my local theatre school and countless near misses in terrifying auditions have all led me to this exact moment.

The first three rounds of auditions the month before had played out as if I were in a dream. My Nan Sylvia took me on the Tube to Hammersmith to visit the Disney offices, where I was thrust into a room full of young, determined and experienced girls, all desperate to get the job. As they loudly discussed their achievements on West End stages and bit parts on *Casualty*, I felt entirely out of my depth. The odd glance over at Nan – sat nearby, visibly desperate for a cigarette yet trapped in this stuffy holding room – was enough to calm my nerves.

WILL YOU LIKE ME IF ...

The day passed in a blur of screen tests and script reads, which I must have managed to execute in a passable fashion. 'You're through to the next round. If you want to take a seat, we will tell you what to do in a moment.' Each time this happened, my eyebrows raised in surprise and Nan's cigarette craving got worse.

As the train sped down the Metropolitan line at the end of the day, our bodies swayed from side to side, my head resting on Nan's shoulder, both of us incredulous at the result of the long day's efforts. My next gauntlet would be a recording of the *Disney Club* TV show, where I would attempt to convince the audience to choose me over the other two remaining girls, to become a full-time cast member. TV shows where winners are chosen by a voting audience are commonplace today, but this was an original concept back in the mid 1990s. I would have to not only convince the audience to like me, but also to bother picking up their landline phones to vote for me. Although none of it feels necessarily natural or instinctive, at this moment, I understand that if I do what is expected of me, I will get a good result. If I behave in a certain way, I will be liked. Not just by the adults I am working with, but also by the audience watching at home.

As the floor manager holds out the fingers of his hand in a widely spread 'five', I know how much is riding on the next three minutes of my life. I want out of my suburban hometown of Eastcote and my monotonous school life. I want to swap the Wimpy on the high street for studio floors and excitement. I want to meet pop stars and immerse myself in the culture I've become so obsessed with.

The floor manager's hand clenches in a fist with only two fingers aloft, which quickly turns to one finger that is swept through the air like a magic wand and then pointed directly at me. The number one in a floor manager's countdown is always silent. Five, four, three, two ... then silence. There are so many tiny details I will need to learn on the job.

I take his visual cue and start to recite the lines that I had pulled together and memorised earlier that day. 'Hello, I'm Fearne. I'm from Eastcote and I love Hanson and Fruit Pastilles.' My smile broadens further as I try to walk down the treehouse steps whilst talking, as I had been directed to do. I reach the bottom, finish speaking and the cameras turn away to film the next segment of the show. Sweet relief floods my body as the adrenalin begins to dissipate.

Unbelievably, I got the job. We had recorded three different endings to the show, one where each of us won. A month or so later, on the morning the TV show was airing, I sat in my front room with my mum, dad and brother. Clenching fists, jiggling legs, biting lips, we sat awaiting the results. When I saw the pre-recorded version of me walk onto the set as the new *Disney Club* TV presenter, I shrieked. We huddled in the middle of the front room, squealing and jumping up and down. It remains the greatest moment of my career. Maybe that sounds a little sad that it's all been downhill from there, but it was to do with the innocence of the moment and the pureness of the reaction. In that moment, I felt liked. It was that simple. I was yet to understand that likeability is as flimsy and ephemeral as a passing breeze. It felt like I'd made it. Today, I don't have any regret or judgement towards my younger self. I'm glad I was naive enough to simply enjoy the high. I didn't yet see likeability as a currency, nor understand what it truly meant – I just felt its warm embrace. All the lessons were learned after this moment of elation. And we will get to those, don't worry.

———

This may sound dramatic and disproportionate, but at times being likeable has felt vital for survival. In my line of work, being liked is the number one currency. When you're a TV or radio presenter, it's almost half the job. Yes, you need to have a certain skill set and an understanding of how to communicate clearly – and with radio presenting, you need to work your way around a complex audio desk – but without the elusive and intangible likability factor, you're toast. Strangers watching and listening to you across the country have to warm to you, feel like they know you, be happy to have you in their kitchens and living rooms as they go about their day. If this doesn't happen, not only might you lose your job, but you could also be personally criticised in the press, and even publicly humiliated and shamed.

Prior to landing my first job in TV, I had very little concept

I BEHAVE?

of what it meant to be likeable. I had my core group of friends at school (who are still my best mates today) and a very basic and simplistic view of what it meant and felt like to be liked. There were some girls in the year above who would sometimes pick on me and a girl in my class who made a point of offering everyone but me her crisps. But I didn't waste too much time thinking about it. I had my friends and that was all that counted. They liked me, I liked them. Simple.

But then I started work and I realised that if I wasn't liked, I wouldn't have a job. That meant I wouldn't have the ability to earn money and I would quickly find myself back in my old life, away from the tantalising studio lights and high-speed excitement. So, figuring out how to make people like me became my number one focus. I might not have been cognisant of this internal shift, and I certainly had no idea how bad my obsession with being liked would get, but the seeds had been planted. I became aware of consciously choosing to behave in certain ways, so that I didn't lose something I valued or miss out on something I wanted. But realistically, the seeds are sown for all of us much earlier.

For aeons, parents, carers and teachers have praised children using the accolade 'good girl'. I've caught myself saying it to my daughter on many occasions and have silently grimaced, wondering how much damage it might be doing. It's always said with positive intentions, but how much are we setting up young women to fail if we are constantly reminding them that life is better (and they are better people) when they are *good*? Of course, with that word comes all the cultural baggage that it carries.

But what does being 'good' actually mean here? If we reduce it down to a syrupy, concentrated, bare-bones mass, then I think we can all agree that it means complying. I have a feeling that *good* in the context of *girl* means to obey and suppress things that are *bad*. If we behave as we are expected to, if we go along with what others want and need, then we are *good*. You are a good girl if you are polite and selfless – quiet, even. I may have called my son a 'good boy' at times too, which is perhaps just as problematic, but I can't help feel that the term 'good girl' is so much more loaded – the expectations seem more sinister – whereas with boys, it's perhaps more open-ended, congratulatory and boosting. Because, of course, there is still less space for young girls and grown women to be outspoken and powerful. Historically, women have had less rights, less opportunity, less people listening to them. We might believe there have been huge, positive leaps and bounds, yet I'm not so sure about that. We live in the hangover era, where women are still fighting for equal pay, opportunities men have had in the workplace for centuries, and the space to show up authentically as leaders. In parts of the world, women are oppressed in ways us westerners cannot comprehend. Speaking to Malala on my *Happy Place* podcast recently was a horrific reminder that so many women out there are silenced and live in constant fear. Plus, the consequences of speaking your mind remain so much more complicated for a woman than for a man. Jane Goodall once said, 'It actually doesn't take much to be considered a difficult woman. That's why there are so many of us.' Women are working in much narrower parameters when it comes to what is deemed to be good behaviour. One step outside of them, and you're considered difficult. So until there is real equality, we should be more vigilant about how and when we are supporting the trope of the 'good girl'.

Living in the confines of the 'good girl' means we swallow a lot of feelings. Most of us will likely have been praised at some point in our formative years for suppressing emotions that actually needed to be released. We may have wept or screeched when we didn't get the ice cream we so desperately wanted. Then, when ordered to stop moaning, we swallowed down the tears and wiped our eyes, only to be told that we were being a good girl for calming down. This may seem harmless and lack the punch of proper childhood trauma, but each time we learn that hiding big emotions is what makes us good, we are being taught to suppress huge parts of ourselves.

Writer and coach Natalie Lue has written an incredible book about recognising and reclaiming your boundaries that challenges much of what many of us learned growing up. *The Joy of Saying No* feels like a much-needed wake-up call. I nodded along reading her section on 'the obedience years'. I don't know about you, but I was a kid in the 1980s and early 1990s, a time when unquestioningly obeying elders or authority figures was normal and expected. As kids, most of us were shit scared of disobeying our parents or teachers. There was a general acceptance that fear of punishment was a good tool to use to correct our behaviour and there was not much two-way conversation between adults and kids to work out why a kid might be misbehaving (exacerbated by a lack of widespread understanding of neurodivergence), acting up, shouting, crying or wanting to do things differently to their parents. This is by no means a dig at generations of parents before me. Times change, culture shifts and – hopefully – things improve. Our parents may have been hit by their parents or thwacked with a belt in class. An act of discipline that was normal and seen as efficient back then would cause outrage today.

But our generation is still slowly climbing out of that hole and is trying to find new ways to cope with the pressures of parenting whilst raising emotionally intact kids. Even though I am attempting to parent differently to the generations before me, I know I've messed up along the way. At times, I've resorted to an outdated approach, asking my kids to behave, stay in line, pipe down, keep quiet. Tiredness, frustration and a feeling of being utterly out of my depth are usually the catalysts for falling back into these habits. Yet I want change – for my kids and for myself. I want my daughter to know she can say exactly what's on her mind and express it when she feels pissed off. I'm not sure I'll ever enjoy being on the receiving end of it, but I certainly endeavour to listen anyway.

I BEHAVE?

Last year, my kids went through a lot of personal change. I'm no perfect parent, but what I did make sure of was that I gave my daughter a lot of space to really tell me how she was feeling, whether it was crying, shouting, questioning me or needing alone time. Rather than calling her a good girl once each storm passed, I made sure to tell her she was allowed to say what she needed, to make noise and to express her anger. I didn't want her learning that she was only a good girl if she made my life easier by suppressing her own feelings.

When our formative years are peppered with rules about how we should behave, it's hard to shake them later down the line. We carry childhood thinking into adult life. We re-establish over and over the concept of the good girl who does as she is told. We firm up those neural pathways that keep us feeling safe because we are playing by the rules. I know that a hefty amount of my actions, or inaction in some areas, are still based on old rules and fears. I'm scared I'll be told off or sent out of class to stand in the corridor with my face turned to the wall. (I've got experience in that one. To be fair, Mr Iggulden was right. Talking about Leonardo DiCaprio in English lessons had very little relevance to *Lord of the Flies*.)

In addition to our childhood conditioning, there is a wider inheritance. For centuries, women have been bound up, tied down and suffocated by harsh parameters that ensure we behave. It doesn't take a history degree to see how little say women have had throughout time and, in parts of the world today, still don't. We couldn't vote, have certain jobs, own a property, drive a car, wear trousers, speak up or disagree with the systems in place. We have had to simply behave.

So many women worked so hard to take power, to change laws, rules and beliefs. But these old paradigms take a while to die out completely. There remains a baseline expectation that we should all want to be mothers (the same doesn't apply when judging a man and his life choices), that we should be the primary care giver (again, a pressure many dads do not feel), that we should settle down and cap our wilder sides (no more dancing on tables, otherwise you'll be labelled a hot mess or irresponsible), that we should be thoughtful and never put ourselves first, that we should age gracefully (whatever that means) – oh, and that we shouldn't age in the first place (more on this one later). These rules might not be written down anywhere, but we certainly feel them on a subcutaneous level.

So, what if behaving in accordance with your own truth, your own set of rules, goes against the grain? How does that make you feel? Trapped? Resentful? More than likely, it makes you deeply uncomfortable. Yet working out our own truth is vital if we want to feel some sense of contentment or, dare I say it, happiness in the long run.

Like most of us, I genuinely don't want to upset other people (although I will have and I will again) and I hold a set of values that determine how I move through my life. But alongside the genuine concern for others is a hidden driving force. One of superstition and social conditioning. One that leads me to

I BEHAVE?

believe that if I'm not good, I must therefore be bad. A rotten egg, a person without empathy and care for others, a *bad girl*. There seems to be no grey area. No room for nuance or pushing boundaries. We have seemingly made being good a binary concept without nuance or fluidity. I think it's this that keeps us nodding, saying yes and smiling so we can retain our good-girl image. However, I'm interested in what sits in the middle. In the canyon between *good* and *bad*, where decision-making happens, self-respect grows and genuine desire is born.

We could blame fairy tales and pantomimes, with their basic-bitch approach to good and bad. You're either Little Red Riding Hood, or the Big Bad Wolf dressed as a granny. Reality TV shows and certain news outlets are today's folk tales. There's the good guy and the bad, and we are supposed to pick the good egg and shout abuse at the bad one. When we are force-fed this two-dimensional view of how humans work, we assume the same of ourselves. We desperately want to be assured we are the good guy or beat ourselves up if we think we are the bad guy. How could we possibly be both?

Yet, of course, we are. We are complicated people with good bits and bad. Every bloody one of us. Even those that appear as sweet as pie. They've called people a cunt in their heads and imagined someone they don't like falling down a well. Everyone has a little bit of the nightie-wearing wolf in them.

We are both because we have an ego. Most decisions in our life are driven by it. It's pretty impossible, unless you're

WILL YOU LIKE ME IF ...

Eckhart Tolle, to move through life without activating your ego. Even if you want to do something charitable or kind for another, there might be at best 80 or 90 per cent of you that is driven by empathy and a desire to help, and then 10 or 20 per cent of you that is motivated by ego and the need to be good or seen as good. Ego, of course, drives the other parts of us that are less desirable (but still parts of us!), such as envy, resentment and jealousy. When our ego feels threatened, the worst parts of ourselves come to defend and keep safe our precious little self-image. Ego ironically stops us expressing the darker side to our personalities too. It doesn't want others seeing the shitty bits, which in turn makes them grow in size and power.

I got very used to being the good girl. My behaviour bordered on martyrdom at times: 'Oh, yes that's fine, I'll do it,' 'No, no, don't get up, let me,' and 'Yes, of course, I don't mind at all.' I would feel detached from the words coming out of my mouth. The emotion behind them was gone because I often meant the absolute opposite of what I was saying. If I felt anger or resentment, I would internally berate myself for not being a perfect little accommodating good girl. What's worse, being honest and saying no and causing a scene, or pretending to be the good girl, yet screaming inside?

I'm not sure I believe in the rules anymore. Do I believe I have to behave like a good girl all of the time just to please others? I don't think I do. Do I believe I have to only show

I BEHAVE?

the best, palatable and acceptable parts of myself to be liked? I'm starting to think not. I've realised that misbehaving can be very fun indeed. It can feel like freedom. When I say misbehaving, I'm not talking about thrashing about, hurling abuse at bystanders or flinging around hurtful comments, or ignoring accountability when it comes to our actions. I'm also not talking about being rebellious or mischievous for the sake of it. Truth needs to lie beneath any act of rebellion.

Truthfully, what lurks in the pit of your stomach? What lies beneath the fear? What do you really want to do? Maybe there is a load of stuff you want to say no to. And yet how often do you find yourself getting in line and doing as you're told – what you think you need to do to be liked and accepted – even when it doesn't feel good? How often do you go to the party you really don't want to attend, just so others don't think badly of you? How often do you park new ideas and desires because you worry that others will judge you? How often do you behave appropriately rather than authentically, just so you don't get slagged off? I often suppress my inner weirdness at the school gates. *Just behave like the other mums. Don't say anything weird. Behave as you should, so you fit in*, my inner voice rattles. I recently read a quote on Instagram that chimed big time. It said: 'You can either be universally liked or authentic. You can't be both.' I love the simplicity of that statement. You simply can't be both. So, which one are you going to choose? We don't have to throw all learned behaviour out the window, but examining the rules we live by, why they were initiated and if we still think they hold up is extremely interesting and at times revelatory. Of course, sometimes there is sacrifice and compromise, moments where we have to make a decision considering those we care for. But life can't be one big compromise. It just can't. A life where we constantly sacrifice our own needs and wants leads to resentment and anger. Trust me – I tried out this theory for years.

Our behaviour has to be rooted in what we believe is best for us. If we have been people pleasing and going along with the rules, then when we start to make some changes, we might piss people off, rock the boat and incite gossip or unwanted outside opinion. And that might feel very uncomfortable at first. I didn't say this was easy. I'm not sure any big lessons learned are a walk in the park (unless it's a park full of dog shit). But don't we owe it to the women that came before us, the generations that had much less say over how they conducted their lives, to live truthfully? Neither of my nans worked, as they were encouraged to stay at home. I often see them in my mind's eye, cheering me on (obvs Sylvia has a fag on the go). We definitely owe it to ourselves and to any younger women or girls looking to us to see how they should behave.

When we start behaving in accordance with our own values and desires, other people will have something to say about it. That one is guaranteed. The good news is that we have options as we deal with the potential discomfort of this. One route is to dissect why that individual (or collective) deems our behaviour unlikeable. What you'll discover quite quickly is that their *why* is not very personal at all – and says a lot more about them than it does you. Do they disapprove of your behaviour because you have highlighted a need for more freedom, one they are ignoring in themselves? Is your challenging of the status quo making them clearly see they are stuck within the confines of their own set of rules? Are they envious? Do they not like change? Do they simply like being outraged? Is your behaviour a huge distraction that they can gossip about in a subconscious attempt to ignore their own flaws and misdemeanours? It could be any of or all of the above, but it's rarely exclusively about you. (They might also just be twats. That's the last option on the list.) So, what are we supposed to do?

What if we just forge forward anyway? View the whole episode as an experiment. In the face of outside opinion, are you resilient enough to still give it a go? What a curious place to find yourself in, I'd say. Compared to the monotony of staying in line like everyone expects you to, I reckon it's far more exciting to try something new and learn about yourself along the way. Pushing yourself outside of your – and other people's – comfort zones will certainly teach you a thing or two about yourself. You may realise you get a kick out of some light-hearted rebellion. You might discover you quietly revel in behaving differently to how you always have. You might find you care a lot less about outside opinion that you feared. We all have so much to learn about ourselves.

WILL YOU LIKE ME IF …

The alternative is pretty bleak. This is the one where you live a life in accordance with everybody else's rule book. A life that suits everybody else but us. I'm not sure how long any of us can happily keep that one up. I certainly couldn't. It was breaking me. It's our life, full of our experiences, and we only get one go at it. So how do you want to behave? And are you willing to give it a go – whether other people like it or not?

Will You Like Me If... I Am Ashamed?

I push through the glass door to the Radio 1 offices and am met with multiple faces that instantly look down at their computer keyboards. No one makes eye contact. Or it certainly feels that way. I feel cold. The kind that lives in your bone marrow. Not even a hot bath or cup of scalding tea could penetrate the iciness that lives inside me.

My body slumps down into an ergonomic office chair and I nod with a half-smile at my producer. He is kind and I know feels empathy, yet he doesn't have the right words to help me. No one does. A senior member of management calls me into his office. A horrible news story that doesn't involve me yet has a tenuous and life-altering link to me will be broadcast on my own radio show again that day. The words he chooses to explain this to me are delivered seemingly without emotion. I can't take any more coldness. I want to cry, but I honestly can't be bothered. I have nothing left to give.

I also feel shame. It's curling up around the entirety of my body like a boa constrictor, quite literally squeezing the life out of me. It's affecting how I walk, talk, dress, sleep, eat. I stare at the floor hoping that if my eyes blur enough, I'll disappear, or teleport back to the darkness of my bedroom at home. *Do not make eye contact*, the shame whispers. Sometimes my throat feels as if it's closing entirely, only wisps of air coming out instead of sound. *Keep your mouth shut*, says the shame. I'm wearing more clothes, in fewer colours. *Hide yourself*, it

WILL YOU LIKE ME IF …

hisses. I lie awake at night, blankly staring into nothingness. *You're not going to sleep again tonight*, it laughs. I either eat to numb myself or don't, as an act of self-punishment. *You're hideous. You don't deserve pleasure*, spits the shame.

I shuffle back to my desk, wishing I could curl up in bed. The last thing I want to do is broadcast to the nation. Looking at the time on my computer, I calculate I have forty minutes before I have to find something to say to over five million people for three hours. *You have nothing to say*, says the shame. *Everyone hates you.* I feel simultaneously glared at, stared at, yet utterly ignored by those in the office. Are they all talking about me behind my back? Or am I a narcissist for thinking that? Only two hours ago, I had dragged myself out of bed, shoulders sloped, the skin around my eyes English-cloud grey. *You don't deserve time off work to recover from this horror story*, the shame shouts. I need to show up, act normal, keep people on side. Stay cheery, stay likeable, keep pushing on.

I feel sick. I'm not sure how I will get through the next few hours, but I hate myself for feeling that way. People would kill for this job. I'm a piece of shit for not being grateful. Buck up. COME ON. Get in that studio and just talk. Open your mouth and talk. Among the fake, breezy pleasantries I'm spouting on the radio sits self-loathing. I don't look up at the nearby monitor with thousands of messages streaming in from listeners. They might consist of the same abuse that's in my head. I shove down the anger, the rage, the sorrow and tears, and I just keep talking.

I AM ASHAMED?

Looking back on this period of my life makes me feel queasy. The memories are blurred with depression and a heaviness that coats everything in a grimy film that stops me from remembering. I can't tell you what happened, as the British press love nothing more than to reignite a story for the sake of a clickbait headline. They don't care about the human behind the story or the life-changing opinions their words create. But I will not be bullied by them again, so I can only tell you what it felt like to have no power because I was drowning in shame.

Shame keeps you quiet and dutiful. It's a straitjacket that inhibits all movement. It's only years later that I feel such rage that I was bullied by the press, treated with very little care by a few colleagues (though many were so lovely, I must point out) and that I allowed myself to be silenced. Now that I'm not lugging around a suitcase of shame, I feel it all. Bring on the galloping stampede of rage, the thumping fists of anger and the torrents of tears. So many tears.

I think the main block for so many of us when it comes to freeing ourselves from being a good girl is shame. While the feeling of others' approval is the carrot that keeps us trying to please, shame is the stick we use to beat ourselves with again and again.

What is shame and why does it hurt so much and keep us hiding in the shadows? The difference between shame and embarrassment is that embarrassment highlights the thing we believe we got wrong, whereas shame tells us we ARE wrong. It's all-consuming and keeps us trapped. It's the voices of others, your own internal voice dialled up to eleven, it's the mistakes you've made illuminated on a cinema screen, it's the feeling you are somehow inherently flawed, unlike everyone else, who is just fine. Shame keeps us handcuffed and holds us to ransom. It sticks to everything and finds a way to infiltrate even the sunnier parts of life.

Having spent years drowning in the stuff, I know why it hurts so much. The pain is often so big and unruly because we feel we cannot find a way around it. We believe what shame is telling us and don't have the energy to fight it. We're trapped: we are in shame and it is in us. *You are bad*, it says. Full stop. That's a cold, hard fact that cannot be fought. It is terrifying to confront shame. You have to be a particularly sturdy woman to do so. And back then, I was not. I believed everything that shame told me I was: horrible, dirty, gross, unsavoury, annoying, pathetic and so on. The list is actually endless. To stand up to that internal stream of relentless internal abuse is very, very hard. It has taken over a decade of therapy for me to do so.

Writing this book has at times been utterly confronting and beyond challenging. I have had to look at parts of my life that I have desperately tried to bury. But you cannot bury any era of your life forever. It'll always come back to bite you on the arse.

Just this morning, I decided to create an Instagram post about shame – and then got shamed by one individual in the comments section. The sting of it made me delete the post.

I AM ASHAMED?

Fuck, I thought I was getting somewhere. Because it's fresh, I want to describe exactly how that shame felt. I'm still sat in a puddle of it now. I feel nauseous, like I've eaten something that's gone off. Curdling, crashing waves of self-loathing and worry knock about inside me. Tension everywhere, teamed with a feeling of utter apathy. The apathy is a faux partition wall between me and the truth of the matter. If I tell myself I don't care about anything, then it will hurt less, right? Wrong! My head is spinning in irregular circles, and I feel like I want to jump out of my skin. I AM BAD. It's the same boring conclusion time and time again. Shame says so, and I believe it.

So, I need to write this chapter more than ever. I need to dive into shame, to bury myself so deep in it that it doesn't scare me anymore. To stare into its putrid yellow eyes and see who blinks first. I have to win this time. I will type it all out, breathe life into the feelings and then let them pass. I will not get stuck. I refuse to take on this random stranger's shame. Their own projection of self-loathing that they are desperately trying to rid themselves of. I don't want it. It's not mine. We have all been shamed, and therefore felt ashamed, at some point in our lives. If you want to rid yourself of it too, keep reading. Let's fucking do this together.

Where it all started in your story will be unique to you, but for many of us, it will have been in childhood. I so clearly remember being the new girl at primary school. Age seven, I had come from a neighbouring town to Newnham school in

Eastcote and was wearing a yellow summer dress, which had been the uniform at my old school, rather than a red one worn by pupils at my new school. I instantly felt like an outlier. In my first English lessons, I asked my surly teacher, who had a walnut whip of grey hair piled on her head, if I could have a rubber to erase an erroneous letter 'A'. 'No,' she said. 'Use brackets.' At seven, I had no idea what that meant. I licked my finger and tried to rub out the offending letter instead. Two minutes later, I could feel her presence hovering heavily by my right shoulder. 'I SAID, USE BRACKETS!' she shouted in front of the whole class. I felt my body tremble. My mouth dried up. I didn't speak or explain that I didn't know what they were. The shame was burning red and it kept me frozen. Considering I don't remember half of my career from the early noughties, it's perhaps unbelievable I can remember this exact moment in full HD. What I was wearing, how my tummy twisted in knots, the way she spat the words out. This shit stays with you. A small moment informing you that you're not safe when you get things wrong. This is the golden rule of being the good girl. You will only be likeable if you get everything right.

I was on a walk with a very good friend last week and we got talking about this exact subject. We don't tend to talk about shame as a nation, as I suppose we assume we are the only person who has it. That's one of the effects of shame's horrid poison – it makes you feel as if you are the only one. But we got into it on this walk and it proved liberating. My friend is

I AM ASHAMED?

utterly gorgeous, an incredibly talented musician and bloody lovely person, yet she surprised me by telling me she often drowns in shame. She admitted that wearing the wrong thing to a party, saying something a little clumsily or simply forgetting an item of clothing the kids need at school will send her spiralling into shame. Rather than feeling a twinge of embarrassment, she jumps to shame. Bam, from 0 to 100. It's the same for so many of us. She will, like me and you, have her own backstory of where that was initiated, but nonetheless, it lives on.

Shame is a bastard. It might start with a life-altering event or have been building incrementally since childhood, but it sticks around and, if you're not careful, attaches to all parts of your life. For women, this often results in making ourselves and our lives smaller. The less risk, the less chance there is of shame. It's one of the reasons I stopped doing a daily radio show. Having had such a horrid experience in those Radio 1 days, my body feels like it's not safe in that environment. If I do fewer shows (I'm now on Radio 2 once a week for two hours), it reduces the amount of risk. Less time on air means less opportunity to fuck up and therefore a smaller likelihood of being shamed. I've shrunk down my opportunities to remain the likeable good girl who doesn't fuck up and therefore doesn't have to feel shame. It's not good, is it?

As my mental health declined in my early thirties, I reduced other areas of my life, a big one being my social life. Bye,

bye friends. See you down the line when I'm a healed, fully formed person who won't mess up every conversation I have. The shame told me it wasn't safe to be out with other humans in case I said something stupid. My own mental arithmetic concluded that to limit shame, I needed to hide at home. It was safe there: no unknown humans I could be weird in front of, only my kids and cats to judge me. Being disliked always ended in shame, so if I stayed at home, I would reduce that risk and not have to drown in shame as often as a result. Of course, it didn't work. Shame follows you everywhere. So, still I was drowning in shame.

But a small life, one where we must never mess up, is no life. Life, true life, includes risk, failure, clumsiness and the spontaneous.

Our cultural inclination is to shame the girl who isn't good. If we can lift our eyes up and away from our own shame, we can notice many female historical figures and see how this has played out time and time again. Recently, I was listening to a history podcast about Marie Antoinette, who was endlessly shamed for her decadence and her supposed promiscuousness, as well as her fashion choices and non-conformist ways in eighteenth-century France. She wasn't playing by the rules, and her behaviour was often shamed, far more so than her husband's. Louis XVI was often indecisive, which led in part to the French Revolution and the fall of the French monarchy, yet who was blamed, shamed and constantly vilified? His young wife, Marie Antoinette. The only surviving

I AM ASHAMED?

child of Henry VIII and Catherine of Aragon, Mary I of England, the first female English monarch, was shamed disproportionately compared to her male predecessors and successors. Nicknamed 'Bloody Mary' for her brutal killing of 283 Protestants, she is one of the most hated women in history and still seen as the evil foil to her half-sister Elizabeth I – yet she was no more brutal or sinister than any man in power since.

But we don't need to look that far back to see the shaming of women. Amy Winehouse was an electrifying talent who charged onto the scene with more charisma than any of her contemporaries. I met her on the set of *Never Mind the Buzzcocks* when she released her first album *Frank* in 2003. She was mesmerising. As she chatted to the makeup ladies backstage, her voice boomed confidently through the BBC corridors. Her body moved with an old-school elegance and streetwise savviness. I was transfixed. Her troubles and addiction were well documented and at times overshadowed her immense talent. Paparazzi took photos of her passed out on benches and newspapers shamed her appearance, weight loss and how she behaved when she was out with her friends and hangers-on. Yet how many male rock stars in history have smoked and sniffed their way through the music scene? The Beatles openly talked about using LSD; The Rolling Stones are celebrated for being debauched boundary-pushers; Keith Moon, The Who's reckless drummer, is remembered as a wacky and hilarious character of rock 'n' roll history. The tone is different. Men's debauchery and chaos is celebrated and seen as exciting, whereas women's exclusively lands them in shame.

Stepping outside of the music industry, we can see how strong, magnificent women like Serena Williams are body-shamed for being too masculine. Her strength has been diminished by ridicule rather than used as a source of inspiration. We must remain quiet, small, calm, considerate and ladylike if we want to eliminate the sting of shame.

Women are often shamed when it comes to sex. To be the good girl and to be likeable, you must be sexy but not slutty. You must not be frigid but also not be seen to enjoy sex too much. These kinds of demands are not put upon men.

A much younger friend of mine told me that for her, at age twenty-seven, there is new dating pressure: where young men are demanding their prospective partners be 'marriage material'. If what my friend sees on TikTok is to be believed, young men want a Pilates princess and a big red flag is seeing a woman dancing behind a DJ booth in a nightclub. WHAT THE FUCK? Have we gone back to the 1950s? Sorry. I have no words. Well, actually I do. FUCK THAT! Young women are being shamed for dancing behind a DJ and showing off their beautiful bodies by dancing sexily. Sod 'marriage material', I call that LIFE material. Get out there and dance, ladies. Dance like no one is watching, yet simultaneously dance in the face of those misogynistic men who need their women tied to a Pilates bench. Dance, dance, dance, without care or shame.

I AM ASHAMED?

Whether it's women wearing too little clothing, exuding sexiness or talking about sex, there is shame. For instance, let's look at the difference in tone and language that has historically been used around masturbation between the genders. Collectively, men can talk about wanking in a jovial, almost cathartic way. Making light-hearted jokes about it and referencing it openly on TV, in the pub or elsewhere is completely normal. Now, I'm a pretty liberal person and am very close to my girlfriends, but I can probably count on two fingers (hmm, surely there's a masturbation joke in there somewhere!) the amount of times I've chatted to my mates about it. We are taught as girls to feel utter shame about giving ourselves pleasure. Equally, there is no space for grown women to discuss it without shame. Good girls don't masturbate.

A few years ago, we had Florence Bark on the *Happy Place Podcast* to break this silence. I could, in my mid forties, feel my face burning as I tiptoed around the subject. Careful as to what I said and didn't in case I was publicly shamed. If you need to break free from years of feeling ashamed when you masturbate, please go back and listen to this episode. Thank you, Florence, for liberating so many of us when it comes to the much-needed pleasurable subject of wanking.

This normalisation of shaming women for their every move has seeped into our subconscious and continues to inform how we judge ourselves and others. Not only do we apply these outdated, patriarchal, wishy-washy rules to our own lives, but to other women's too. Whether it's the mum at the class Christmas party who gets that bit more pissed up than everyone else, the celebrity who has an opinion or the relative that breaks free from the norm, we judge and we shame. Lumping someone else into the shame-heap may momentarily reduce our own internal shame, but it never lasts. There is only one way to eliminate shame, and I'll come to that shortly.

Shame makes most of us very scared of our *bad* side, or shadow side. It tells us that we must be benevolent at all times. Even if we are prepared to acknowledge our shadow side, we often don't feel safe enough to show it. We show the portions of ourselves that we believe are good, pleasing and acceptable. We tend to shun the bad bits altogether, in fear that if they're uncovered, people will run a mile and then shame will set in further. But getting to know our shadow side is essential if we want to feel deep self-compassion and really understand ourselves. It's also important to reveal those parts of ourselves to our loved ones, as it gives them an opportunity to truly know and see us.

Right, head torch on, sleeves rolled up. Let's take a walk into my shadow. Oh, yes, as expected, shame. This is a big one for me, and one I'm constantly working on in therapy. Because I had a huge period of my life swallowed up by shame, sometimes that part of me still attaches itself to whatever it can grab hold of: past mistakes, regrets, bad choices, harsh criticism from others. Shame Velcros itself to anything

I AM ASHAMED?

it rubs against and can send me spiralling into self-loathing. I don't like to show that side of myself and until recently couldn't even admit it was lurking in the background. This is another reason why it's important to shine a light on these parts of ourselves. When we ignore them, they grow in potency and power. When we acknowledge them, they quieten the hell down.

Oh, hello, ruthlessness. Another part of my shadow I don't like to think about, yet there it is, sat stubbornly staring at me. It's always been there. I don't necessarily like it, but I can see it. I can be, and have been over the years, ruthless when I have something in my sights. I will crawl to the finish line to get the job I want. I will ignore those around me to get the results I am after. I will grit my teeth and push and push until I have it in my hands. I would love to be softer, gentler, slower in my approach to life, but that's honestly not the case. I can either ignore this part of myself and suppress it, or I can accept it and recognise when it shows up, so I can decide what to do about it.

OK, let's keep walking, past the piles of regrets in the corner, until we come to envy. It's glowing green in the murky shadows and pulsates with potency. Most of us have this one; we just don't like to admit it. On days where my confidence is waning and I feel beaten down, I will cast my eyes to the left and right and see how everyone is doing so much better than me. Their kids are in more after-school clubs and reading much more complex books. Their houses look picture-perfect and all their plates match. My peers are getting bigger numbers on their podcast episodes and fanfare that I could only dream of. Everyone looks better, younger, more graceful than I do. At best, I stay in the self-pitying phase, and at worst, envy turns into anger and frustration. Or it gives rise to a competitiveness that serves nobody, driving up from the gut to deliver cruel words and incite gossip and judgement.

Oh, but wait. Look up ahead – here comes self-righteousness. Wow, it's galloping towards me like a smug stallion, its head held aloft and tail swishing wildly. *I'm better than you*, it says in a whine. *I would never do that*, it confirms. It's a part of my shadow side that I really do not like. It makes me feel grubby, and paradoxically leads to a lot of self-loathing, yet nonetheless, it's there.

There are more parts to my shadow side we could meet and greet, but you get the point. We just cannot be perfect all the time. Having bad bits to your personality doesn't make you *bad*. It makes you human.

Do you dare look into your own shadows to see what's lurking? Remember, we all have one. What do you think is skulking in your shadows? What do you not like to admit, look at, notice, within your own personality, backstory and emotional baggage? What are you covering over with people pleasing and the expression of being a *good* person?

Recognising these parts of ourselves doesn't mean we give into them. If you notice you have shame in the shadows like I do, shining a light on it will not make it more present in

I AM ASHAMED?

your life – ignoring it will. When we have awareness and apply some healthy curiosity to the equation, we can start to understand ourselves better. We might not need to pathologise every single action, reaction and emotion in our lives, but getting curious about why these parts of us exist allows us to slowly let them go. I'm not naive enough to believe that one day I will be shadowless, as life is far too uncertain and complicated for that, but I do believe we can heal parts of ourselves so less lurks in the shadows – and what is there has less power to hurt us or take the reins and start calling the shots.

Through therapy, I have realised the shame I carry is not mine. It belongs to others. Mainly men. Men who have shamed me, treated me badly and left me lumbered with it. Male journalists who have said horrendous things about me. Men who have degraded me on social media. Men I have dated. I refuse to carry that shame. Sorry, chaps, it's not mine. Don't want it. It's not serving me. I don't need to be the good girl to be valued and accepted. In fact, I'm a fucking woman, now you mention it. It goes without saying that there are some incredible men in my life too. Men that have helped me love myself, guided me through tough times and championed me. This is not an attack on men. I love men. But I cannot have this conversation without addressing the shame I carry and who has cast it upon me.

Who does your shame belong to? If you don't know, don't worry. Knowing the origin isn't imperative to healing from it. You just need to remember it's not yours to carry anymore. Give your shame a silly name. Call it 'Sugar Tits', or 'Cunty', or something else demeaning. Reduce it to a silly voice that you won't listen to. I know that may not instantly erase it from your life, but it's a good little exercise to practise. Hear it as a squeaky, whiny voice that almost bores you it's so obvious. *Here we go again*, I tell myself. That irritating voice of shame.

Although I still have bouts of feeling shame, of hearing that nasty, critical voice, I don't drown in it anymore. I don't believe I am bad. I refuse to believe I am flawed beyond repair. I will not let others bring me down by shaming me. These days, I know when I've actually messed up. It's never fun, but at least I can recognise it, choose to pick myself back up, try again and make better choices. Messing up doesn't make me, or any of us, inherently bad. It makes us human.

One surefire way to move through shame is to talk about the things that make you feel ashamed. Shame breeds in silence. As long as it stays in your head, it'll grow in volume and density. It is never comfortable talking about parts of your life or a story that makes you ashamed, but it's a damn sight better than it all living rent-free in your head. Each time I breathe life into a story that makes me recoil with shame, it slightly backs off. Saying it aloud, not running from it, and having a level of acceptance dilutes shame bit by bit.

The other miracle that occurs when you share your story of shameful moments is the person you're talking to will have

I AM ASHAMED?

theirs too, which they might share in turn. By opening up, you give them permission to free themselves from shame too. Of course, you have to pick the right person: someone you love and trust. When you feel ashamed, it is hard to believe that even those who love and adore you will be judgement-free, but I promise you they will. Shame is trying to block you from saying it aloud.

Not long ago, I was putting on my best face to someone new in my life. I was utterly terrified of them seeing anything other than the fun, light-hearted, easy-breezy, humorous side of my personality. I imagined if they knew some of the darkness that lived in my head, or saw me spiral when my thoughts turned ugly, they would run a mile. This fear built up momentum until I couldn't ignore it anymore. I found myself in a negative thought spiral in their company one weekend and opened up. Each word stuttered out of my mouth, syllables wonky and croaky. But I got there in the end. I managed to string together half-sentences to explain how I was feeling and the root of why I sometimes spiralled. I was shit scared they would think I was insane. Rejection loomed in the background, humiliation waiting around the corner. But neither arrived. My broken sentences were met with hugs, kindness and understanding, and now that person knows me as a whole human, rather than just seeing the parts of me I'm happy to show to anyone. It's not easy, nor comfortable, but this process allows others to know us fully and to recognise their own shadow sides as well.

WILL YOU LIKE ME IF …

None of us should be living in shame. Life is too short to waste another second hiding away because shame is telling you to do so. Talk to someone you love about the things that bring you shame. Know that we all have a shadow side – even the people that are very good at pretending otherwise. Having a shadow side, making bad decisions, having bad thoughts, or acting on them does not make you bad. We all fuck up and get things wrong. We are fallible humans who are trying our best. You are not bad. Repeat after me: YOU ARE NOT BAD. And you don't need to be the good girl either. So if we aren't bad, but aren't the good girl, what does that make us? I would say somewhere in between. Beautifully complicated women.

Will You Like Me If ... I'm More Like You?

I'm twenty and full of wild experimentation. As I walk out of the hairdresser's, I know I've made a grave mistake. I'm weaving through the harried shoppers in Harrow town centre, self-consciously smoothing one side of my hair down whilst keeping my eyes to the pavement. On the drive home, I try not to make eye contact with myself in the rearview mirror. On one hand, I do have that little buzz of feeling like someone else, which I love. With each new pair of shoes, lipstick shade or piercing, I get closer to being someone different. Or maybe an iteration of myself I'm yet to explore. It feels good, expansive, and each time I believe this one change may solve all my problems. Yet, although I feel the tantalising tingle of this yet-to-be-discovered version of myself, I also feel foolish. Deep down, I know I've dyed my hair black at the back with a bleach-blonde strip at the front because I want to be liked by the cool gang. The cool gang are the glittering indie scenesters who fill the pubs and bars I go to after work. They have cigarettes hanging from their plump lips, jeans slung low on jutting hip bones, and a half-smile that never progresses from a smirk. I want in.

I've just left *Diggit*, the weekly kids' TV show I've hosted since I was seventeen. I'm young enough to be seen as childlike but I long to be and feel grown up. I'm caught in a limbo, where I'm hosting the odd kids' TV show alongside the cool, indomitable *Top of the Pops*, which remains the height of zeitgeist cool. I have one foot in a ball pit and the other is putting out a fag with my DM boots. I'm mostly confused. Kids' TV feels safe and familiar. I've outgrown some of it, but I'm also looked after by a chaperone and kind-hearted TV producers and know how it works. This new world of *Top of the Pops* and the odd appearance on entertainment programmes like *Never Mind the Buzzcocks* feels like I'm zooming down a motorway without a seatbelt on.

I'm now invited to cool gigs and spend my evenings rattling around pubs in Camden and small venues on Tottenham Court Road. The boys have early 2000s fringes swept to one side and they wear band T-shirts and skinny jeans. The girls smell like freedom and wear their off-the-shoulder T-shirts like superhero capes as they suck on menthol cigarettes. I want to belong. I want to be liked. But I don't feel how they look. Their cool exterior seems to bash harshly against my goofiness. I'm too chatty and enthusiastic and I know I'm being too eager to fit in. But I can't help it.

There are two girls who seem to be the epicentre of the culture. They're called Mairead and Tabitha and their DJ moniker is The Queens of Noize. A whirlwind of chaos surrounds them, as bands fumble to get closer to their magnetic auras and the party follows wherever they go. I look on, watching how they cartwheel into rooms, piggyback each other to the DJ decks, fringes falling over sultry eyes and grins showing mischievous teeth. If only I could be as cool as them. If only I could be as popular. All the girls want to be them; all the

I'M MORE LIKE YOU?

boys are in love with them. In this music scene, in this corner of London, they are beyond likeable. They are *IT*.

When I'm near them, I can feel their intoxicating and infectious energy radiating in concentric circles that draw everyone in. I stand on the sidelines, in my try-hard clothes that are a mash of influences, as I try and work out who I am in the world. I feel clumsy, too self-aware, extremely uncool. I'm an observer rather than a participant, and certainly not the instigator of the social scene like they are. Although I won't admit it to anyone, I want to be adored by the cool boys in bands. I want songs written about me (this did happen to Mairead and Tabitha on more than one occasion) and for the girls to admire me. But my immaturity and lack of self-worth lead me to imitation rather than inspiration. Rather than find my own place in the scene, I just straight up try and look like the girls I am in awe of. I'm all rock 'n' roll exterior with a soft, nerdy interior.

I walk through the door of my little cottage in Harrow and stare at the unrecognisable person in the mirror. I had imagined this hairstyle would make me feel invincible, that I would somehow instantly possess the sophistication and confidence I desperately want. It turns out, I just feel a bit silly.

I can look back and not feel silly now. At forty-four, I can take that version of myself by the hand and smile at her softly.

WILL YOU LIKE ME IF ...

Though, saying that, I do still wish I'd had the guts to be truly myself aged twenty. To know that I would have been more readily accepted if I had shown up as myself. Mousey blonde, zero edge, zero hip bones, highly enthused about everything, still secretly loving pop music more than indie and very uncool. I didn't feel then like that version of myself, the real one, was very likeable at all. But I look back now and I do really like her. She had determination and grit about her, a life already full of stories and adventure and a willingness to see the good in everyone. I wish I'd had the strength to preserve my natural enthusiasm and hadn't so readily blunted it to appear cooler, like those around me. I tried to erase little, suburban, un-edgy Fearne and tried to build a new one, just to be liked.

In an attempt to be likeable, we have all, somewhere along the line, tried to be like those around us to fit in. It's human nature to want to feel part of something, but often we forgo our own sense of self entirely to do so. Travel back in time to your first few weeks at secondary school. Thrust from the safe cocoon of junior school, all of a sudden you're in a place where there are new rules, new teachers and new kids.

At the tender age of twelve, I clearly remember wanting to find my tribe as soon as humanly possible. I ended up in a group of seven girls who are still my closest friends today. We were a swarm of hormones, fancying the same boys, putting on the same Heather Shimmer lipstick, wearing the same Kickers shoes to school, and copying each other's mannerisms and cadence of speech. To this day, outsiders look at our gaggle and comment on how our voices are one sing-song of northwest London chatter. We wanted to be liked by each other so we merged into a slightly different iteration of the same person. Our own identity, passions and irritations were bespoke, but our dress sense, speech patterns and senses of humour started to merge into one homogeneous movement. I copied Lucy's handwriting style, Hayley's lilac Head sports bag, Becky's pulled-back ponytail, Ally's laugh, and so on. We were each bits of one another.

This is all part of growing up. We were trying to figure out how to be young women, and so we bounced off each other. And the truth is that, as social creatures, staying in line with those around us feels easier and safer. We might support the same football team or political party as our parents or friends because we feel a sense of camaraderie. We might like the same music as our close friends and bond over those bands or DJs. We may dress in a similar way to those we socialise with. It's easier to conform, nod along to other people's ideas, vehemently agree on world issues and gossip about those that seem different.

However, there is a deeper root to mimicry. Yes, we want to be liked, accepted and part of something, but, as humans, we also have a physiological need for closeness and meaningful communication that we seek through imitation. We mimic others to be close to them, and to assure our place in the group. Whether this is valued by the other person or even understood is a gamble. We mimic, then hope. Hope we are accepted. Hope we are liked.

The psychology of mirroring is so ingrained in our society that you can see its reverberations everywhere. Trends would not exist unless we had this desire to be liked by others. When I was twelve, did I really want a perm with a straight fringe (I doubt it) or was I just copying the fashion models I saw in magazines so everyone at school would like me more? When I was thirteen, did I wear Buffalo trainers completely autonomously? Or did I want all the other girls at my dance school to think I was cool like them? Did I buy a rugby-style jumper last week because I really like it or because a friend of mine who is particularly stylish looked incredible in it and I sort of want to be her? Obviously, the latter. We are constantly influenced and subtly shown what to wear, eat, say and think by those around us and by society at large. It's also how herd mentality works and echo chambers thrive. When there are big narratives driving the political or social landscape, it can be hard to go against the grain. For fear of exclusion, we can find ourselves mimicking those around us and hijacking their opinions rather than taking the time to dive deeper and form our own.

It's not necessarily a bad thing. It goes without saying that forming an allegiance with like-minded people in the name of activism is an incredibly powerful force. Finding your tribe and gathering strength in numbers is what creates positive change. Yet there is danger on the flipside, where

I'M MORE LIKE YOU?

certain groups are unwilling to hear counter-arguments and get stuck in corners of the internet that deliver constant reinforcement of their beliefs via algorithms, leading to division and narrow-mindedness.

It might seem like I've travelled away from our original question, Will you like me if I'm more like you? But it all comes back to a fundamental need to be accepted. We form alliances and converge our ideas and thinking to feel that we belong. We want to be liked and embraced, but of course that can be by the wrong people and for the wrong reasons. Our egos don't always mind who is doing the embracing or why, which is how we end up in toxic friendships, following the wrong crowd or having a perm.

The majority of the time, we are not conscious of how much we are mirroring others around us. It can be so subtle. A hand movement here, a scrunch of the nose there. The recipient of the mirrored behaviour then starts to subconsciously trust the person imitating them. There's familiarity and safety in reflected behaviour. I've noticed how often I cross my arms when talking to someone who is doing the same. Or I sit back and slouch if the person I'm talking to is. We mimic to feel like we belong. We mimic to be likeable. It's human nature.

This all starts in childhood. We watch our parents laugh, shout and cry, and learn how to move through the world accordingly. When we are tiny children, we naturally seek that level of connection, whether our parents are present, kind or attentive to us or not. Our little brains and nervous systems just want to feel safe and loved. So, we seek approval by mirroring their behaviour in a multitude of ways. Yet this subconscious and innocuous mimicking in childhood can trip us up later down the line. For example, copying how your parents react to stress or adopting their unhelpful coping mechanisms can take some serious unpicking later in life.

I can see how I picked up my mum's need for excitement pretty early on. Seeking the big highs in life became second nature, as I had consistently seen my mum strive harder for better and look for fun when there wasn't much in sight. I also learned to react in a big and expressive way when stressed out, as that's what I often saw. From my dad, I learned to find the stillness in the chaos where possible but also to want the comfort of home and bed in an urgent way when the sun starts to set. Like Cinderella, both my dad and I start to panic when the clock strikes 10pm. Like everyone, I've mimicked and established patterns of behaviour through observation. Can you notice those patterns in yourself?

We don't usually continue to feel the same need to mimic our parents' behaviour into adulthood – we have, by that stage, more than likely established a relationship with our carers that is based on verbal communication (plus, a lot of our teenage years were probably spent trying to defy them and make our own way!). But we never lose that innate urge to mimic those around us. In fact, not doing so can feel scary, to the point where we feel reluctant to challenge the status

I'M MORE LIKE YOU?

quo and find ourselves going with the flow, even when it feels wrong. Because it still feels safer.

When you have a different point of view or don't want to play along with existing dynamics, it can cause tension and conflict. When we think and behave more intuitively, those around us have to learn to interact with a different side of us than they might have previously seen. No longer mimicking, or imitating, means that they don't have the comfort of seeing their own familiar reflection beamed back at them.

Have you ever faced a big decision while trying to navigate the terror of thinking, *What will others say? How will they react? Will they still like me?* I'm sure we can all think back to one of these moments in our own story. Have you left a job that was deemed a stable one? Exited a relationship when others thought it was going swimmingly? Found yourself yearning for a new hobby that no one saw coming? Take a moment to recognise that decision and how much strength it took to action it. Where there's change, there is usually uncertainty and a big fear of rocking the boat.

When I left Radio 1, I was told by nearly everybody in my life that I was making a huge mistake. It was a coveted job on a show with millions of listeners and brought lots of work opportunities. But I knew I had outgrown it. Not in a grandiose way, but I had stopped wanting to learn. That's always a sign for me to move on. When I'm no longer yearning to learn, I gotta get out. Some people judged me, some talked shit about me, some were eventually really pleased for me.

WILL YOU LIKE ME IF ...

Of course, if you are the only one in your family or social circle who sees things differently or is unwilling to conform, then you may feel ostracised. That is never comfortable, but I believe it's still less dreadful than suppressing your true beliefs. The alternative is to keep mimicking those around us and stay in our lane. To stick to the job that's making us miserable. To remain in the unfulfilling relationship. To never let ourselves try new things because of what others might think. But if we are constantly striving to be the good girl who doesn't rock the boat, we get stuck. Moving away from what others expect from us to what we actually want is freedom, but with it may come outside commentary, often judgement and sometimes dislike. Although going against everyone else's opinions is discombobulating, I think it is always a healthier option to move through the world in an authentic way.

If you find yourself on the receiving end of other people's negative opinions about a decision you've made for yourself, you need to get the magnifying glass out. It's time to look very closely at each individual and see what their own projection is. What are they putting on *you* that belongs to *them*? Are they envious that you've had the guts to leave a job you're unhappy in because they are unhappy in their job? Are they outraged that you've left a relationship because they feel trapped too? Are they bitching about you trying a new hobby because they're too scared to step out of their own comfort zone? Are they taking your actions to be a criticism of their choices? It's rarely exclusively about you. If you've stopped mirroring someone, or simply refuse to continue conforming, feathers will be ruffled.

But life here on planet Earth is short. The older I get, the more I understand this and feel it in my bones. If we are living our lives for other people – to appease, to please, to comply, to placate – then we are going to end up with a bag full of resentments and regrets. I truly believe that it's far better to live life according to you and your values and take the risk of being disliked.

The biggest lesson I've learned from being disliked or judged is to have my own back. Nobody is coming to save you. Others may be able to help and hopefully you have some amazing mates who can support you, but at the end of the day, you have to save yourself. In moments where it feels as if everyone is judging you, or hurling abuse, it's time to really put this into practice. Can you have your own back when nobody else does? I have been forced into stepping up like this on many occasions. When looking for outside approval stopped working, when my chips were down and I realised I couldn't rely on the applause of others, I had to cheer myself on. In these moments I may not have recognised it as cheering myself on, but the fact that I got out of bed each day suggests a level of self-compassion. And the big changes I have made in my career also emphasise a level of self-care I've gotten better at exercising. Cheering yourself on doesn't mean literally getting pompoms out and jumping about, shouting your own name joyfully. It means making better choices, looking after yourself, eating well, cultivating a gentler inner voice and not giving up on yourself altogether.

So, what does it take to make decisions that are based purely on what you really want, regardless of whether it'll buck the norm or not? I think it's based on trust. Trusting in life. Trusting in the lessons you've learned. Trusting that no single outcome is without its value. Even when we are judged, accused and ridiculed, there are rich lessons and gifts received.

Of course, it's easy to say but not always easy to do. Do you trust in life? Do you trust that with every road bump, there are valuable lessons learned? Do you have hope for the future? Can you muster up optimism when things are going badly? Do you trust in your own ability to see things through? I'm not sure many of us do. The anxiety epidemic we are living in suggests that most of us do not trust life one bit. We assume the worst thing will happen, that we will be hurt or betrayed and that life is ultimately full of pain. During my lowest period of mental health in my early thirties, I didn't trust much at all. I had been screwed over, hurt, judged, trolled, and left feeling very alone. Sadly, when we experience outcomes like this, we end up in a bit of a cycle where we attract more of the same. In an attempt to protect and defend ourselves, we build even higher walls to keep others out. We then have even more evidence that the world is a brutal place and that we cannot trust anyone.

But what I've learned as I've spent years crawling out of a dark hole is that there is plenty to trust. There are people we

I'M MORE LIKE YOU?

can depend on, those that will not judge, and lessons in it all. I've also learned that you can be hated and still be OK. You might have heard people utter the phrase 'trust the process' and felt irritated because you're keenly striving for the end result: the bit where you're safe, out of the woods, through the mountain of pain you're feeling. To trust there is hope at the other end can feel utterly impossible, yet it's not. It is completely possible to not only gather lessons as you move through tough times, but to also find newness and happiness down the line.

Trusting in life doesn't mean that everything is going to turn out peachy. There will be twists and turns, unexpected tangents and the odd turd-shaped gift, but we can keep the faith that we are on the path we are supposed to be on. When we experience injustice, for instance, we might find it particularly difficult to find any good lessons learned or a silver lining of any kind. Yet if I had given up trusting in life when I most needed to, I know I would still be stuck feeling bleak and hopeless. Trusting is what gets us out of a rut and allows us a slightly different perspective. It's what allows us to take the path that feels right to us regardless of outside opinion.

Do you want to do things differently to those around you? For women, this question is huge. There is so much expectation on women. To have children, to be a nurturing carer to everyone, to excel at work because we supposedly now have the chance, to be gracious, sexy, gorgeous, sophisticated, intelligent, wholesome. But what if you don't want any of that?

WILL YOU LIKE ME IF ...

What if you want to make up the rules and create a life that works for you? When those around you are conforming (even if that is totally right for them), it can feel almost impossible to go against the grain, but maybe, just maybe, you'll get a huge kick out of it too. Even if it means being momentarily unlikeable or not understood.

Breaking the stereotypes that have kept women quiet and conforming is a minefield. You'll find yourself not only judged by disgruntled men but also by women (as we've been brainwashed by the patriarchy). If you decide you don't want children, someone will have something to say. They may even try and change your mind. If you decide you want to be a full-time worker while your partner is the primary caregiver, people will talk. If you dare to dress differently to the women around you, you might be ridiculed or questioned. There is always going to be noise when you are a disrupter. People don't like disrupters. They like peaceful conformism. They are reassured to see their choices mirrored in others. Yet, the older I get, the more fuel I have to ditch prehistoric ideas of what it means to be a woman, and the more excitement I have for what that means.

But the vital question is: how do you want to live and how do you want to feel? You can't cap true wants and desires forever. It'll catch up with you. It did me. Although I don't regret all of the madness my twenties delivered, I do regret some of my choices. I was boundary-less. I looked for validation from the wrong people rather than the ones that already loved

I'M MORE LIKE YOU?

me. Beneath my emulation of the cool kids around me, I just wanted to like myself. Not believing I was likeable just as I was led to an eating disorder and some grim relationships. In my thirties, I wanted to say no to certain people and situations but instead stayed in line and let frustration and anxiety build. In my early forties, I wanted to break free from the often back-breaking, all-consuming role of being a woman with kids, a job and so much responsibility. Rather than asking for help, I would often make assumptions about how other women were coping with their lot and copied them. Keeping my head down and lugging all my responsibilities around more than likely didn't support my physical health. I ended 2024 with an operation to remove a tumour from my face. Now, the latter may not exclusively have come from me people pleasing, but I know a large portion of it came from stress. People pleasing is fucking stressful. It creates omnipresent tension that you become very bloody used to. Tension in the body creates stress in the body and that stress has to go somewhere.

And yes, when you stop people pleasing and put yourself first, stop mirroring those around you and forge your own path, you'll perhaps cause upset, but it's still the better option. Be you. Don't be like everybody else just to fit in. If you follow others because you feel lost in your own life, understand that they don't know where they're going either. No one has a clue. So be lost in *your* way, not somebody else's.

Look to those who have disrupted before you. Every woman who has chosen to do life their way has created a path for others to walk down. Every woman who has bucked the norm and dealt with the fallout has created a little more space for us to do the same. We can all see these women. They're dotted throughout history like volcanoes erupting with flowing lava that creates new avenues for the women that came after. Pick your favourites and be inspired by them. There's no need to emulate or imitate. They wouldn't want that for you. True mavericks lead the way for positive change yet leave you enough space to do your own thing.

Personally, I'm grateful for women like Annie Nightingale, who barged into the male-dominated world of radio and made space for all of us who came after. She not only held her own but cultivated her own style and influence and gained respect and love from music-industry insiders, bands and artists along the way. She didn't need to pretend to be a man to do so. Nor did she stunt her own femininity or vivaciousness to fit in. I imagine that it wasn't easy at times, but thank God she did. I sat next to her at dinner a few times when we were both at Radio 1 and she had so many stories, so much determination and passion. It was utterly contagious. After her came a flurry of other strong, brilliant female DJs: Jo Whiley, Zoe Ball, Sara Cox, Clara Amfo. I mean, imagine a world without Jo Whiley. No, thanks. Who are your heroes? Who can you look to and see how they blazed their trail?

Remember, this one short life is yours. You don't have to get it right all the time or pretend that you don't care what anyone else thinks. We do care – it's natural. Did I learn to stop trying so hard to fit in with the cool kids and be brave enough to be myself? It took a while, but yes, I did. But have I still felt confused all over again about fitting in as I have gone through different phases in my life? Of course! For example, I remember standing in front of my wardrobe on my son Rex's first day of school, wondering what a school mum was supposed to wear. As if it were a character to play. I put on a long-sleeved T-shirt with a gilet over the top. Where else would I wear such a getup? Nowhere, that's where. I wanted to blend in, look like the other mums, be seen as a dedicated school mum. I ditched my own sense of style of mismatching bright colours, for something bland that said, 'I'm a school mum.' Luckily, that phase lasted all of a week before I became exhausted by the idea of playing dress-up each morning. I can look back now and recognise that standing at the school gates is enough to make even the sturdiest of individuals doubt themselves. In a sea of women I'd never met before, I just wanted to fit in.

It's so important to remember that your actions don't have to align with those around you. Your mannerisms, dress sense, job choices, life choices, relationship choices don't have to sit within the status quo. Find like-minded people and dive into the deliciousness of belonging – but never to your detriment. Don't shrink, pretend you like something or echo opinions just to be liked. Find what makes you tick and buck the norm. How bloody exciting. I'm feeling buzzed up writing this chapter. I might go and do something reckless, like

WILL YOU LIKE ME IF …

get another tattoo. So many untattooed people have something to say about that. I've been told I'd look better without them, that I look as if a child has drawn over me, and that the tattoos are unsightly. Well, my dears, I couldn't give a fuck. I love them. I don't need to look like everybody else to feel likeable. And neither do you.

Will You Like Me If ... I'm Perfect?

I leave my dressing room at BBC Television Centre and make the short walk to the studio, my Converse trainers squeaking on the shiny floor. I love the curved corridors that circle the inner sanctum of the building fondly known as The Doughnut. Built in the 1950s, seen from above, it resembles an Earth-dwelling USS *Enterprise* from *Star Trek*. I spent my childhood longing to go there. Every episode of *Live & Kicking*, the Saturday morning kids' show that was a linchpin of the weekend for children, teens and hungover students alike, was filmed at Television Centre. I wanted desperately to walk through the big glass doors to the reception and interview pop bands in Studio 1.

Now aged twenty-two, as I push through the heavy swinging doors to the next section of curved corridor, I still feel that buzz of being at the BBC. I'm about the age Zoe Ball would have been when I was watching her on *Live & Kicking* back in my parents' front room in Eastcote. Still, I often feel bemused that I've managed to make my dreams come true. It's been several years since I landed my first job in TV as a teenager, yet there are still moments when I feel I've teleported into the TV directly from my suburban front room. Working in TV is just as exciting as I'd hoped, even more fast-paced and high-octane, but there's also the mental turmoil I wasn't anticipating, the imposter syndrome, the insecurity.

WILL YOU LIKE ME IF …

I thought I was meant to feel complete once I had 'made it'. I thought I would feel perfect.

I walk onto the studio floor, the hushed quiet of the empty set making my whole body tingle. The squeak of my trainers on the black polished floor is the only sound to break through the silence. Camera operators and floor managers glide around the studio, setting up for the next shot. I run my lines in my head again. My memory is now so used to quickly learning a script, then clearing it to make way for the next one, that I barely have to apply any effort. I stand on the appointed spot. I smile as the red light on the camera beams. Pillar-box red, signalling for me to be alert, ready, perfect. There is no room for error. There are plenty of people – who are just as hungry as I was for my first job – always waiting in the wings to replace me. Critics poised to leap on any small mistake. The pressure is omnipresent, so much so that I'm almost unaware of it. It's normal. A coat I wear every day, so familiar in its fit and weight.

The makeup artist steps in to check my face. Squinting slightly at the eyeliner she applied moments ago, she takes a thin brush to reapply one section of the black flick I've become accustomed to wearing. 'There, perfect,' she says. The director says in my earpiece, 'There are a few strands of hair sticking up on your left.' I press my palm to my scalp and flatten them back down so they're undetectable to the human eye. Subconsciously, I suck my tummy in, a reflex that kicks in as soon as a camera is on me. I smooth my top down over

I'M PERFECT?

my now flatter stomach and wait for my cue. Being on screen illuminates any tiny defect, imperfection, stutter, crease, lump, bump, mispronounced word. The audience picks up on every minor detail. I'm programmed to notice them before the audience can.

On the outside, I'm shiny, glossed, brushed, buffed, fluffed, sucked in, rehearsed, primed for perfection. But what nobody knows is that I've just been sick in my dressing room. I'm in the grips of bulimia and it's my dirty little secret. I want to feel empty, light, purged. I want to be perfect, like all of the pop stars I interview. Being exposed to svelte pop stars who have flat, smooth stomachs and glistening shoulder blades has brought a new hyperfocus to how my body appears to the outside world. As a teenager, I had round thighs from years of ballet, a little pot belly from giving in to my sweet tooth and a muffin top that popped over the sides of my too-tight flares. Bulimia seems like a way out of being trapped in a body that doesn't mirror what I see around me. I want to be perfect, too.

Sadly, back then, I just didn't know that hurting yourself and damaging your body to force yourself into a certain body shape is far from 'perfect'. I assumed that if I looked like the women I looked up to, I would be liked and nobody would be able to see that I was just some random girl from the suburbs.

I spit out the chewing gum I've been frantically working around my mouth so the smell of sick abates. I've already sprayed perfume over my clothes. I smile down the barrel of the camera. I am jolly. My makeup is perfect. My body is incrementally shrinking, along with my sense of self. What I don't realise is that nobody is perfect. I truly believe that everybody around me has their shit together and feels as if they belong. They are perfect and popular, and they know it. I don't take the time to look beneath the surface of the overly styled outfits and slick early noughties hair to see what is really going on. I have no clue if they are happy or like themselves. Even though I am part of the mirage created for television by makeup artists, stylists, lighting and camera angles, even though I know that what I feel inside doesn't match what I am desperately trying to project on the outside, it just doesn't occur to me that other people might be feeling the same way. I think it was our old friend shame again, telling me that I was uniquely 'wrong'.

It still astounds me how we can make so many assumptions based on what we see, and yet have no idea what is really going on inside someone's head. Having now interviewed countless pop stars, actors and well-known personalities on my podcast *Happy Place*, I know many of the people I had previously put on a pedestal were in fact feeling the very same insecurities.

Perfection will look and feel different to all of us, but there is one guarantee: it is exclusively elusive. We will never properly feel perfect. We may touch the edges of it in brief moments, when we nail a presentation at work, get our kids

I'M PERFECT?

through a temper tantrum successfully, like the reflection we see in the mirror on a good day, but largely we will be tortured with the idea of it.

What do you think about when I say the word 'perfect'? Do you relate it to how you look and appear to others? Do you need others to see that you are living perfectly? Or do you need to feel like you are on your A game every day – punctual, precise, pragmatic? Do you need to be the perfect wife, sister, mother, friend, co-worker to everyone around you? The pressure we put upon ourselves is insane.

On top of this ungraspable fantasy, we can assume everybody else *is* nailing it. We notice other people's supposedly perfect lives, bodies, relationships, work achievements and feel like we are failing even more. We dangle a carrot in front of ourselves that says, *If you're perfect, you'll be popular. If you're perfect, you'll be liked.* Which, of course, is all utter bollocks. We might even know in our heads that it's total bollocks. But the idea of 'perfection' still has a hold over many of us in different areas of our lives. But we'll get to that in good time.

How often do you look around and create a narrative that places others above you? How often do you assume that the other parents on the school run are living the perfect life? Who in your eyes has got it all sorted? Most of us create some kind of hierarchy in our social lives and families in an attempt to work out how we fit into it all, but it's mostly nonsense. We have no idea how anyone is feeling on the inside, or what shit they're covering up, unless we take the time to find out.

WILL YOU LIKE ME IF ...

Having been a perfectionist for many years (now perhaps a very slowly recovering perfectionist), I know that those tendencies to compare my insides with others' outsides really ramp up when I feel the most out of control. The ship is sinking, the storm is a coming, the shit is hitting the fan, so I become more controlling and in need of superficial perfection. I'll plump sofa cushions, reply to every email in my inbox, bleach the sink and restyle my hair, all in an attempt to convince myself that I'm OK. What I've learned the hard way is that 'perfect' can't save me. It won't guarantee that everything will work out just fine and it won't make me more likeable – particularly not to myself.

I believe we've become even more accustomed to view an outward expression of perfection as a meaningful marker of success, and this is especially thanks to social media. We are bombarded with online images of perfect homes with labelled glass jars and colour-coded snack cupboards, bodies on beaches, bronzed and bouncy, and other people's kids wearing matching outfits eating homemade, kale-infused after-school snacks. If, when scrolling through this pit of picture-perfect paradise, our own homes are a shit tip, we feel bloated and gross and our kids are screaming at each other whilst mainlining ultra-processed crap, we may start to feel pretty shite about ourselves. All of a sudden, amongst the ubiquitous perfection, our normal starts to look anomalous and a bit bleak. We apply this madness to how productive we are and how

I'M PERFECT?

we look, socialise and parent. The relentless comparison to people we know, and others we don't know and will never know, holds the potential to drive us to pursue an all-round perfection that is unreachable.

We are also living in a system where this level of perfectionism is celebrated. The click of a little love heart beneath each photo allows us to quantify how *liked* something is, reinstating the notion that perfect equals popular. You probably have read about how the social media 'like' button was initially meant to be a tool to spread kindness. Letting others know you appreciated their posts seemed a fun and innocuous way to spread some joy. Yet, as we all know, over time, our perception of this innocent little love heart morphed into something quite different. It's now a status symbol, a way to make money, a means to supposedly quantify our worth. Even though I intellectually know that the amount of likes a post gets has no bearing on my actual value as a human being, I can still get caught in the trap of believing the hype. My ego swells at the rising numbers on a popular video post but my heart sinks when another has bombed. I know how this works, yet am still dangerously sucked into the vortex of undulating self-worth evaluation. But when we aim for perfection, we often miss the opportunity to be authentic. That might mean losing our true quirkiness, ignoring our flaws that help us to honestly connect with others and shutting off entire parts of our personality.

WILL YOU LIKE ME IF …

One of the greatest pressures on women throughout history has been to look perfect. What this entails has obviously morphed and changed throughout the decades as trends wax and wane, but the pressure is omnipresent none the less. Whether thin eyebrows are in or out, bigger bums are lusted after or shunned completely, or waistlines are to be cinched in or not, the pressure to follow the ever-changing rules is constant.

When you're on the TV, those pressures become magnified and can easily lead to near obsession. Although my eating disorder could have been instigated by any number of events in my life, I'm pretty sure being on the TV from a young age (and in the nineties – God, it was mad sometimes) was conducive to a huge amount of body dysmorphia. If I'm entirely honest, I can still hear the hum of it today. I'm not free of body dysmorphia, that's for sure. From my mid teens, I was regularly on set with TV monitors facing me, my reflection omnipresent. It's hard enough as it is to not obsess over body image growing up but having that constant reflection nearby meant at times I thought of little else. In those formative years, I assumed that if I looked like I wore expensive perfume, was sophisticated in a way I assumed came from a level of discipline I didn't naturally possess, then I would be more likeable. I viewed my body as a problem I needed to fix and chose an entirely unhealthy way of doing so. I didn't view my eating disorder as a mental health problem; I simply saw it as the only route to a body I longed for. Yet, of course, I didn't become more likeable. I ultimately ended up liking

I'M PERFECT?

myself a lot less in the process. I was lost in a cyclone of self-loathing and body battering.

In the past, I closed down parts of myself that I was worried would lead to others not liking me. Instead, I put on a show. I plastered my face in makeup, smiled inanely and was overly chatty to cover up the sense of self-loathing. I hid feelings of insecurity behind a supposedly 'perfect' career. I ignored anxiety and kept it locked away, while inviting guests into a home that looked orderly and perfect. It's all pretty normal stuff. Most of us have done this at some point or another, if not regularly. We don't always believe that being our authentic, perhaps tired, slightly quieter (or louder), messier selves will be liked. I'm also certain that over the years other women have looked at me and assumed I've got my shit together. Assumptions may have been made about how together I was, how perfect my life was. The same assumptions I've made about women around me. If only we were brave enough to lose the veneer of perfection and tell each other that in fact we feel a bit lost, or a mess, or aren't coping very well at all.

Strangely, insecurity seems to be a direct path to the trap of perfectionism. It's the finger that prods the wasp's nest. It jibes and whines, inciting a deep need to cover flaws and supposed wrongs, so the outside world only sees the good bits. But if we have the self-knowledge to understand that insecurity is what is fuelling our perfectionist ways, might that allow us to view those whom we deem perfect slightly differently? If the version of themselves they are presenting to the world is so unfailingly poised and glossy, maybe they haven't got it all sorted? Maybe they feel so flawed that they are working overtime to only show the perfect parts of themselves in the hope they'll be liked and accepted by others. Maybe the shininess covers shame or parts of themselves they are scared of.

However, we have to be careful not to judge people when we perceive inauthenticity in someone's outward veneer. Because – being honest with ourselves – how often do we ridicule those who only show the 'perfect' parts of themselves, of their lives? How quick are we to jump on the bandwagon of having a pop at someone in the public eye who is too polished, too considered, too nice?

Sure, this is partly because we have become utterly bored of seeing online perfection, with its high-resolution filters, staged photos and dinners made mindfully with manicured nails, but we also try to tear these people down because we are cross. Even if we don't totally buy it, we are still annoyed that we don't feel perfect. We are riled that our lives, in comparison, feel like a mess. We are livid that we aren't perfect. So, here's the crossroads where *perfect* incites anger and sometimes even hate. What we thought might bring popularity, acceptance and adoration actually may bring the complete opposite. We want to see other people living messily; real lives make us feel connected. It makes us feel OK in our own mess.

So, perfection often creates a huge disconnect – a canyon between the imperfection we can see in our own lives and

I'M PERFECT?

what we assume of other's lives. Or a suspicion or resentment that someone is 'pretending' to be perfect. The veneer of perfection we perceive in others stops us from properly seeing them at all. We are sold the idea of perfection by, well, pretty much anyone who has something to sell, but we crave authenticity.

Now I'm in my forties, I am much more willing to show multiple sides of myself. It took me years to feel comfortable talking about bulimia, but now I can look back at that version of myself with deep compassion. I knew no better. I can calmly say sorry to my body and also forgive myself. I wouldn't make those choices now knowing what I know, but it made me who I am today. It's enabled me to have deep empathy for those in the grips of an eating disorder now – for anyone who is struggling to like themselves in the face of some of the damaging messages society still sends us about what we should look and be like. And it has ultimately encouraged me to thank my body for recovering so well and working healthily today.

I am also far more comfortable admitting when I've gotten things wrong. I'll show you my huge eye bags. Tell you about the times I have actively hated myself. Moan about how I've not slept more than three hours because my head was whirring. I'm over pretending otherwise. I'm not a perfect mother, friend, daughter or sister, nor do I make all the right decisions or act like the best version of myself all the time. If anyone does not like me for any of the above, I have to assume that they're not aware of their own imperfections, or that my own mistakes or messy parts remind them of their own. To remain sane in our complicated, imperfect lives, we must try and cultivate kindness to ourselves. My best and very wise mate Clare once said to me, 'Just don't turn the gun on yourself.' This has stuck with me. Other people can judge me, dislike me, even hate me, but as long as I don't turn on myself, I can still find a little room to like myself.

I know you already know this, but I feel the need to re-iterate that it's imperative we learn to like ourselves. If we can like ourselves amongst the messy, sloppy, chaotic, imperfections we all house, then we have a much better chance at feeling and being all right. It means we can stop striving for perfection and just be OK as we are. I'm going with the word 'like' rather than 'love', because let's not run before we can gently jog without getting insanely out of breath. If I quizzed a random selection of people from the contacts in my phone now and asked, 'Do you like yourself?', I'm pretty sure most people would answer by saying either 'not really', 'a bit', or maybe even 'on a good day', at best. I'm not sure there are many people I know who would emphatically reply that they really jolly well love themselves.

I think there is a pervasive sense that how much we are allowed to like ourselves is dependent on what we manage to achieve, rather than who we know ourselves to be. Society today is big on achievement. Whether it's hustle culture,

I'M PERFECT?

a general emphasis on winning at life, or the now quantifiable popularity on social media, we believe achievement is the key to self-love. So when we have stuck to the workout plan we said we'd do, nailed it at work, finished the chores, made a nutritious dinner, only then can we feel OK. But what about in the imperfect moments? When we are just about managing, when we didn't finish our to-do list or are tired and ratty? Or in the total stillness of idleness. Can you like yourself then?

And what about the times when we have behaved badly – let someone down, gotten something entirely wrong? For most of us, it's so much harder, even impossible, to like ourselves then. When we have fucked up, we often assume we are the only ones to have done so. It's not often that people want to shout about the times they have royally messed up, as we usually privately drown in shame and regret, then never talk of it again. But the good news is EVERYBODY has fucked up. Every single one of us. We have all made the wrong decision, said the wrong thing, acted from a place of jealousy or anger, been selfish, hurt other people. We've done so because we are human and life is bloody complicated.

When we can truly land on the notion that imperfection is a universal trait and part of the human condition, we can rid ourselves of some of the isolating shame and start to look for forgiveness – not from others, but from ourselves. If we want to even attempt to like ourselves, then we need to forgive ourselves first. We need to forgive ourselves for every moment we believe we have acted imperfectly, and let the shame go. You can even try saying these words out loud to yourself: 'I'm sorry, please forgive me,' which is the start of a Hawaiian prayer of reconciliation and forgiveness called *ho'oponopono*. It ends like this: 'Thank you, I love you.' You can say it quietly to yourself or think of others that you know you need to privately apologise to as well.

Practising the art of forgiveness opens up space for us to like ourselves. It might not happen straight away. We may be too conditioned to only see our imperfections and wrongdoings, but in time, this thinking becomes more natural and space opens up for self-compassion. We'll dive deeper into self-love (or self-like) a little later on.

Remember, perfect won't save you. Other people won't like you more if you're perfect. You're not a robot that's here to get it right all the time. You're a human who is trying, experimenting, attempting, learning and growing, and that kind of growth is full of beautiful imperfection. Embrace your imperfections and you'll not only like yourself more but that energy will also radiate from you, attracting others to try the same and to connect with you on a much more authentic level. We are all perfectly imperfect.

Will You Like Me If ... I Keep My Mouth Shut?

I walk into the spacious boardroom for about the tenth time and smile broadly. The beige mac that I'm wearing is tied uncomfortably at the waist and feels like a fancy dress costume rather than something I'd like to wear in front of millions of people on the TV. One of the producers looks up from her phone, which she is frantically typing on, the harsh overhead lighting illuminating her furrowed brow. 'No.' She swats me away like a fly, without making eye contact. My jaw clenches and I walk out to the corridor to try on another coat. There are perhaps thirty more coats hung uniformly like sardines on a metal clothes hangers. This time, it's a stiff denim trench coat that feels like I'm wrapping myself in cardboard. I shuffle back into the boardroom, tens of unoccupied office chairs face in different directions, the one occupied chair moving slowly from side to side as she keeps her eyes on her phone until she hears me enter the room. 'No,' she says again, then goes back to her phone. This tiresome parade continues for what seems like hours. A new coat, a slightly different iteration of the word 'no', I leave the room, then return. In my head, I'm screaming, *I'm a TV presenter, not a model! Let me choose my own bloody coat. No one watching will care. Also, I get the feeling you are fucking with me. Are you? Is this a power trip?*

But, of course, I don't say any of that. I dutifully change coats until we land on a cherry-red PVC trench that she seems to quite like. I'm still in shock that I've got the role of

WILL YOU LIKE ME IF …

presenter on a prime-time TV show on NBC in America. Millions of people will watch, and opportunities could present themselves. I am in my mid twenties and full of the American dream. I cannot speak up or say that this coat parade made me feel foolish. I keep quiet. I keep smiling. I want to be liked.

One of the producers on the show (who I'm sure has taken an instant dislike to me) started her fuckery the evening before. She had taken me and the director for a meal at a steakhouse. I had talked at length in my initial interview about my vegetarianism, which began when I was ten. We had gotten into a discussion about it and the cuisine back home in the UK. Yet there I was, sat at a table with my only food option being fries, while large slabs of raw meat were brought to the table for her to choose from. *Do not complain*, I thought. *Do not bring up yesterday's discussion. Comply. Keep your mouth shut. Be likeable.*

Isn't it funny how our people pleasing really kicks in when we know someone doesn't like us? Someone gives us the cold shoulder, and that makes us want to impress them even more. We so desperately want them to see we are worthy, and we believe that if we win their acceptance, we'll feel good about ourselves. So, rather than walking away, protecting ourselves or not caring, we try harder. Though, maybe you don't. Your

I KEEP MY MOUTH SHUT?

defence mechanism might be to close up to protect yourself from rejection, but I was most definitely on a personal mission to get this woman to change her mind about me.

But for the duration of the filming of this one-off show, which saw incredible people break world records live on TV, she made my life difficult. Whether it was changing the script last minute, asking if I could host the show with an American accent on the day of the broadcast (thank God I did speak up and contest this one, as the thought of footage of me existing in which I'm transatlantic-drawling my way through a live TV show makes my vagina curl) or attempting to take the red PVC trench coat straight from my trailer for herself. (Luckily, she was intercepted by the stylist, who told her that I was to keep it. Thanks, love – although I've since given it to charity in a much-needed detox of anything related to toxic memories.) Yet I remained mostly silent and smiled at her whenever she walked by, eager to please, desperate to be likeable. Yes, I was only twenty-six and it was my first TV show in America. And I think it's natural and often right to show a level of respect for those older and more experienced. But this was something else. I could smell it coming off her. The need for power.

I made it to the end of the live show and felt I had done a good job. I kept my British accent – although I was told I had to say the word 'tuna' with a hard T, rather than the British 'ch': 'Toooona'. I felt ludicrous doing that, but again, I was too scared to say otherwise. I was proud of myself for

WILL YOU LIKE ME IF ...

getting through it, but part of me felt diminished and worn down by her constant need to control my every move. The funny thing is that even though I kept my mouth shut and did as I was told, I still got the feeling she didn't like me at the end. So, all in all, my silence and attempt at winning her over were futile.

Looking back, I have compassion for that younger, less experienced me who was too scared to speak up. I wanted this woman to like me – and that meant keeping my mouth shut and going along with her rampant dictatorship. On this job, she was my boss, so I wanted her approval deeply. I don't think I could have played it any differently at this young age. I lacked the robustness of proper self-confidence and was worried any contesting would lead to a telling off. I still hate being told off to this day. If someone says, 'Can I have a word?', I feel my arse dropping out of me. Retrospectively, I can see we were both driven by fear: she was afraid of losing control and I was afraid of being rejected.

If we go back to the big question we started with – *why* do we need to be liked? – we can perhaps recognise that insecurity so often sits beneath it all. Trying to win over a surly and distant person might be an easier, quicker route to self-love and acceptance. Surely if the person who doesn't quite get us starts to see our brighter, brilliant side, then we will too?

If you've never tried to win someone over in this way, then do not worry – I've tested out this theory for you. I might not have won over that authoritarian TV producer, but I've

I KEEP MY MOUTH SHUT?

successfully chipped away at standoffish types and spun around in circles for dismissive, cool people, slowly winning them over. But did I feel any better about myself deep down? Had the deeply rooted fear of rejection completely dissolved? Nope. I may have diluted that fear for a few weeks or months, but its suppression is short-lived, fading over time like perfume does. If anything, the act of trying to win others over is utterly draining. If I'm putting on a bit of a show for someone, or purposefully keeping quiet so I don't ruffle feathers, I can feel my energy levels slipping away, as if my soul is being sucked out of my nostrils with a straw.

When we keep our mouths shut, we show up as an entirely inauthentic version of ourselves. We forfeit our own personality, feelings and words in an attempt to be liked. Yet when we do this, the other person isn't getting to know the real you. Instead, they're getting a watered-down version. So, if you do convince them to like you, it's not necessarily *you* they like, anyway. It's the performance you're giving that they're responding to – or your submission to their ideas and their need for control. Over the years, I've heard myself saying things I wouldn't normally, have stayed quiet when I disagree with someone and have said yes when really I mean NO WAY. I've pretended to like beatnik poetry and Morrissey (I sat through a whole gig at Wembley for that one), and I have eaten fish even though I'm vegetarian because I was too scared to say what I really wanted. It was all in an attempt to be likeable to those around me.

WILL YOU LIKE ME IF …

How often do you keep your mouth shut so you don't suffer potential embarrassment or ridicule? How regularly do you swallow down words that you would really quite like to say because you don't want to rock the boat or risk someone disliking you? We've all done it, so don't beat yourself up. Being aware that you're doing it in the first place is step one on the ladder to caring less about being liked. We'll get to the other rickety steps as we continue through this book, but first, I want to tell you just how bad things got for me. I seemingly took the question 'Will you like me if I keep my mouth shut?' to the absolute extreme.

Perhaps this sounds odd, as starting in my teens and for the entirety of my adult life, I've had a platform to speak up in front of many people. I was paid to talk. It might not have always been my words that I was speaking aloud, but I had a platform nonetheless. And being a broadcaster of course comes with great privilege. At times, I've been able to talk about issues I'm deeply passionate about and start conversations I've felt were needed. For that, I will always be grateful. But in my early thirties, I found that very privilege to be a ball and chain around my leg.

Presenting a radio show is one of the most intimate ways you can communicate with an audience. It's your voice in their ears. Your words in their car. Your stories in their kitchen. It can be the most beautiful way to connect with your listeners and I was lucky enough to have experienced so many moving moments in my time at Radio 1: having a cry hearing

I KEEP MY MOUTH SHUT?

Adele sing 'Someone Like You' for the first time in the Live Lounge, welcoming countless babies on air when new mothers messaged to say that they had pushed their newborns into the world during my show, or reading out my goodbye note I had scribbled after ten years at Radio 1, a lump the size of a golf ball in my throat. Listeners would text in with their thoughts and stories, and we would often laugh and cry together. What a joy those moments of connection were. But – and there's always a bloody but – there is a dark flipside to this intimacy, and it's incredibly hard to deal with.

As a floating voice emanating from a speaker, you are often dehumanised and used as an audio punch bag. People who are having a tough day or are generally unhappy have the freedom to take out their anger on you. I've been called every name under the sun, told I'm annoying, too cheerful, too complimentary after every live performance – and have been told to simply shut up, to leave and also to die. In any other context, this would be described as bullying, but when you're in the public eye, apparently it doesn't count.

During a period of very low mental health, numbed from the daily antidepressants, and yet still feeling battered by the onslaught of press intrusion and noise around me, I found the toxic messages came even thicker and faster. I was not in a headspace to cope. Each one would burrow through any hope or positive thoughts I was attempting to cultivate and set up camp at the forefront of my mind. They started to eat away at my confidence and self-esteem. As a result, everything that came out of my mouth was overthought, contrived, reduced down to the bare minimum. I stopped trying to be funny, I limited how much of myself I gave away, I diluted my personality to a weak imitation of the person I used to be. And then I quit. I stopped talking altogether. I believed at that point that the only way to be liked was to silence myself. Although I don't regret leaving Radio 1, as it led to so many incredible new paths and opportunities, I feel sad that I let those voices in. Their comments weren't the sole reason for me leaving, but they were the reminder and simultaneously the instigator of how badly I thought of myself at the time. I actively silenced myself to save myself.

Have you done this? Have you stepped away completely from something or someone because you were scared to speak up? Or because there was no room for your voice? Or because you felt unlikeable? How did that make you feel? It's OK if it makes you angry, sad or maybe even feel indifferent and numb. I have been through each stage: feeling sorrow, self-pity, rage and burning fire in my belly to indifference and occasionally compassion toward those that feel the need to hurl abuse.

Although we can't control other people's actions, what they say or if they like us, what we can do is notice the autonomy we have. I didn't think I had a choice back in my radio days. I assumed that I had to leave the door open for any opinions to fly my way. I had no boundaries in place and no self-protection from constant outside opinion. Not only

I KEEP MY MOUTH SHUT?

did I subconsciously welcome all commentary, I also believed it. If Carrie from Carlisle thought I was stupid, I believed it to be true. If Shaun from Shropshire thought I was irritating, I believed it to be true. I started to conflate my own ideas about who I was with total strangers' fleeting judgements. I didn't speak up or stand up for myself. I kept quiet and got smaller. But we do have a choice. We can choose whether to let the comments in and we can choose if we want to believe or dismiss them.

Humans are naturally social animals. We are wired to learn from others and to want to know what other people think. It's just part of our makeup. But we also all have the autonomy and judgement to decide whether someone's feedback is helpful or based in fact. This is baked into us too. Sometimes we just have to practise exercising it.

I used to get stuck at the point of feedback. The searing pain of someone's nasty comments would stick with me for days or, at worst, years. You know when you go walking in the park in the summer and you brush past one of those hitchhiker plants with the little balls that cling to your clothing and seem impossible to get off? Well, I was walking through meadows of negative commentary picking up those pesky, sticky balls laced with abuse. Those comments would then start to inform how I acted, presented myself and how much I would say out loud. I got trapped in a state of mind where I suppressed the pain yet shrank because of it, which led to a lot of self-loathing.

WILL YOU LIKE ME IF ...

Acknowledging the choice we have as to whether we take outside opinion on does not mean suppressing the feelings. Negative words and opinions hurt. We will still feel the sting, the pinch, the gut punch, but we can decide that that's where it ends. However, if we don't allow ourselves to feel the pain, we can't heal from it. Feel it, heal it.

Previously, my process would involve feeling the pain then revisiting it constantly, exhausting myself and losing my sense of who I was. If something went wrong in my day, I would pull out a horrid comment from the Rolodex of past abuse in my mind and torture myself with it. Equally, if something great happened, I would reach for that time Barbara in Burnley had called me a twat, and remind myself not to be too happy or chuffed with myself. There were always nasty comments to draw on and I was relentlessly reaching for them and drinking them down like vinegar. All of it pulled me closer and closer to silence. It didn't feel safe to speak.

These days, now that I have an understanding of the pointlessness of that torturous method, I feel the pain, then let it go. I choose not to dwell on it or drown in it. So how can we get to this point? What tools are available?

It can be helpful to look at the data. Cutting through opinion and other people's projections leaves us with facts. Solid facts that we can label 'life data'. I have evidence that I'm not a twat, as Barbara suggested. (Can I point out that Barbara doesn't exist? No Barbaras were hurt in the making of this book.) I can recall times where I've been helpful, kind,

I KEEP MY MOUTH SHUT?

thoughtful. I have proof that I'm not entirely stupid, as Carrie from Carlisle had suggested. (Carrie doesn't exist either.) I have written books, run a business, succeeded in areas I had no idea I could. I have evidence that I'm not entirely a moron, as Shaun thought. (Shaun ... OK, you get the point.) I have made mistakes like all of us have, but I seek to understand where I went wrong and learn from that. We all have tons of data that shows more accurately who we are and what we are made of – hard facts that cut through the noise.

Looking back to the big question in this chapter – will you like me if I keep my mouth shut? – you might prefer that I don't say certain things aloud, or on social media. My opinions or thoughts might not align with yours. You might like me less for speaking up. That is all true. But it doesn't mean I shouldn't speak up. And the same goes for you. It's up to you whether you silence yourself or say what you believe should be said. Will *you* like you if you stay silent, if you allow the opinions of others to shut down your voice? If, like me, you've been criticised for speaking up, or simply speaking at all, you may find it very hard to feel you have a choice, but you do.

There are other reasons why we find ourselves staying silent. For example, how often do you find yourself bursting with ideas but are too scared to tell anyone about them or share them at work? Maybe you even want to change your life entirely, but feel too terrified to tell anyone your plans. What if your words don't land well? What if your ideas are scoffed at? What if everyone laughs or talks about you behind your back? We can spiral off into the land of 'What if?' forever if we're not careful, and end up unnecessarily taking a back seat. The thing is that, yeah, others might laugh in your face or think your ideas are bad, but that isn't a good enough reason to keep quiet. Creating something new or changing direction means there will be risk. Very few good ideas are immune to risk and outside opinion. If you want change, want to create something different, want to give something a try that sits outside of the status quo, then there's always going to be a danger it might not go the way you hoped. Speaking up almost always creates uncertainty, but it shouldn't stop you.

Those who taunt or knowingly cause others embarrassment by mocking or undermining their ideas or thoughts usually feel a lot of fear about speaking up themselves. They're the ones who expend energy judging others rather than bravely putting their own ideas forward. If we bear this in mind, we can ask ourselves why we want to be liked by those who judge rather than celebrate others. Why are we keeping our mouths shut to avoid commentary from those who are too scared to take any risks themselves?

I have taken a lot of risks over the years, and do you know what I have found out? Embarrassment won't kill you. I've said stupid things out loud and been ridiculed. I've spouted out ideas that didn't land in a room full of people with befuddled faces. I've tried new things that haven't worked out. All of it is embarrassing, or at times humiliating, but at no

I KEEP MY MOUTH SHUT?

point did I drop down dead. Sure, some of these have haunted me in moments of solitude at 3am. Some have stayed with me and like to pop into my brain at the worst possible time. But there are many others I have managed to laugh at down the line.

What we need to remember is that everyone has these moments. We have all said clumsy things, voiced a shite idea, said something mad. There are no exceptions. But there comes a point at which it's almost boring to bash yourself over the head with these historic faux pas. What a yawn-fest it is to remind ourselves of these long-gone moments again and again. Instead, we can choose forgiveness. We have to forgive ourselves and let ourselves off the hook. If we don't, we might feel tortured by the feeling of humiliation for long periods and stop talking about our ideas aloud. This might sound bleak initially, but we will all be dead in 100 years. Those times you called someone by the wrong name, said something a bit stupid, came up with an idea that didn't land, will be forgotten. It won't be your lasting legacy. Not trying at all is far worse than trying and being embarrassed that things didn't turn out as you'd imagined. Regret is much more uncomfortable than the sting of humiliation.

Speaking our ideas into existence is key. Yes, we have to have the ideas in the first place and it's essential we work hard to bring them to fruition, but we also need to use the power of speech to conjure them. In my first novel, *Scripted*, one of the characters, Jackson, explains the meaning of the word 'abracadabra' to his friend Jade, who is struggling with people pleasing. Jackson tells her that it's an ancient Aramaic word that means 'I create as I speak.' That's why magicians use it at the end of a magic trick (in the 1980s, anyway. Not sure I've heard Dynamo shouting it out before he walks on water). If we want to create, we need to have the idea, speak it aloud and then get to work. If we keep our mouths shut purely because we are scared of failure and embarrassment, we'll never create anything. All great creators have stepped over the threshold of potential embarrassment to make something brilliant. Every great book you've read, poem you've imbibed, song you've adored, speech that's fired you up has been created by someone willing to take the risk of being disliked.

Think about Taylor Swift's 'Shake It Off', if it helps – a song that explicitly dives into her previous fear of being disliked and her newfound liberation in not caring quite so much. Listen to the opening verse and you will hear her directly explaining some of the misconceptions people have about her, from having nothing in her brain to dating too many men. Rather than keep quiet and take the judgement from others, she chose to call them out and remind them that she would be shaking off any further commentary indefinitely.

A lot of the time we may not realise the level to which we are silencing ourselves. This stuff traces right back to our childhoods. We might have been told to 'shut it' by a parent, to 'keep quiet' by a teacher, or been called a 'big mouth' by a friend at school. These micro moments add up and can

I KEEP MY MOUTH SHUT?

create a low-level anxiety that becomes our normal, right through to adulthood. Who told you to shut up as a kid? Are you still holding onto those words? If you can recognise that you don't need to carry that opinion around anymore, you might try a way to let it go. Visualise a box in your hands with their words inside. Set it down by your side. Or write down the name of the person who told you to keep your mouth shut, how they said it and how you felt. Then burn it outside, tear it into tiny pieces or scribble all over it. I love the act of ritual. It always feels like a tangible and powerful way to move on from old history you want to let go of.

In Louise Hay's book *Heal Your Body* (a book I recommend to everyone), there is an index at the back with causes of many illnesses and ailments, and affirmations to repeat to help treat them. Under throat issues, it lists the causes: 'The inability to speak up for one's self. Swallowed anger. Stifled creativity. Refusal to change.' When I was diagnosed with a throat cyst in 2019, that paragraph could not have been more of a gut punch. The words articulated exactly how I felt. I had been swallowing down words that desperately needed to be said. Often, they weren't spoken aloud because I was scared of being disliked. That refusal to speak up led to immense resentment and anger. I wrote about this in depth in my previous book *Speak Your Truth*.

The affirmation that Louise Hay recommends when you have been swallowing your voice is, 'It's OK to make noise. I express myself freely and joyously. I speak up for myself with ease. I express my creativity. I am willing to change.' Saying those words out loud to myself, whispering them into the darkness before I went to sleep each night, felt like liberation. I was freeing myself from the handcuffs of keeping quiet in order to people please. It may sound utterly unbelievable, but after weeks of thinking about how much I was keeping quiet, how many words I was swallowing down and how I could indeed change, the cyst naturally dispersed days before I was due to have surgery. It may have been a coincidence, sure, but I do believe my change of outlook and willingness to rectify how much I had been suppressing helped the tension release in that area of my body. Whenever I feel myself going mute in the presence of a big personality, or feel scared to say my bit, I remember that little cyst. I think about the thousands of words that I gulped down over the years and how keeping quiet didn't save me from being disliked but instead led to a health scare.

This might sound contradictory to everything I've just said, but since writing *Speak Your Truth*, I've also learned that there are times when silence is golden. This is different to being afraid to speak up, because this kind of silence is chosen rather than enforced or born out of the fear of being disliked. It's a silence that states that you're not willing to engage in an argument or discussion that doesn't align with your thinking. I can be hot-headed and, on many occasions, have fired off an email or text angrily because I felt it imperative to let

I KEEP MY MOUTH SHUT?

the other person know how wrong they were and how right I was. I saw it as freedom of speech and a mechanism for self-defence. But now I know that sometimes it is appropriate to say my bit, like if someone has got the wrong idea about me, but on other occasions, I make a choice to stay silent so as not to expend energy in a detrimental way.

If I know that my words won't be heard because the other person is blinded by anger or judgement, I don't need to say anything in that moment. It's then my job to find some acceptance of the lack of control I have in how others see me and to understand that there's not much I can do about it. If people are gossiping about me or making assumptions and I'm certain their minds cannot be changed, I will choose to stay quiet and find some semblance of mental peace, knowing the full truth of who I am. You can say a hell of a lot by saying nothing at all. When silence is a choice that leads to peace rather than a shrinking of self, it can be very powerful.

So how do we work out when it's right to say something versus staying quiet? What is the difference between keeping our mouths shut and choosing to stay purposefully quiet? I believe keeping our mouths shut comes from fear. We keep quiet to appease and not upset others. Whereas choosing to stay quiet comes from a place of empowerment. Choosing to remain quiet more than likely means you have deliberated for some time and have concluded that your silence speaks volumes. The choice might have been made because you know your life will be less drama-filled and more peaceful mentally.

Equally, when we choose to advocate for ourselves and speak up, we are pushing past the fear of what others will think and say. So, it all boils down to choice. Do you feel you're choosing to stay quiet or have no choice in the matter as you are sidelined by fear?

At times, we need to speak up and advocate for ourselves. When we are being treated unfairly or are simply in the habit of acquiescing to another person's demands, something needs to be said. The outcome might not initially be that fun to experience. Your words may be met with hostility or irritation, but that's better than feeling long-term resentment towards someone else. The outcome may be messy in the short term, but you can see that it leads to mental peace in the long run. Speaking up in this instance is vital. Never easy, but you can level with yourself that it's going to be better for you.

Then there are other occasions when saying your bit will be the equivalent of throwing a hand grenade into an already agitated scene. If you are in conflict with someone whom you cannot find a middle ground with, it's unlikely that hurling harsh words their way will fix much. Fighting fire with fire won't lead to long-term peace for either party, so in this instance, is staying quiet a more peaceful option for you? Only you can decide. But if we think of the long-term outcome, we will have a better idea of how best to communicate.

I want to round off this chapter by asking you to think about what you're not saying. When you say yes to that thing you

I KEEP MY MOUTH SHUT?

really don't want to do, what is it that you really want to say? Is it a vehement, succinct no? Is it an exhausted 'not right now'? Is it an angry 'fuck off'? If the latter chimes with you, it doesn't necessarily mean you have to say 'fuck off' aloud, but it is beneficial to realise the emotion behind your true response. There is nothing wrong with feeling angry. Getting in touch with how you're really feeling will only give you more clarity on what you want and don't want. You can then firmly and clearly say no and know you mean it. If you've recognised your own anger first, you won't have to express it in your response. Firm and clear. So often I've ignored the inner anger, then either stored it up and felt physically wretched, or covered it over only for it to explode out of the seams later down the line. Which it always does. When I recognise my anger, I can then privately vent it and address it before I respond. I don't always manage this perfectly, but it is my aim.

What about when you're in a meeting or group and you have an idea but keep silent? What is it that you're not saying then? Is it 'Listen to me, I have something to say'? Or 'I have an idea. I'm nervous to say it aloud, but I'm going to anyway'? Once you've had some time to think about that, ask yourself why you are staying quiet. Whether it's because you don't want to make a fool of yourself, or piss people off, or incite anger, underneath it all, you'll probably find a fear of being disliked.

So, as you move through the rest of your day or week, notice the moments when you're holding back what you truly want to say. Ask yourself why. Stare the fear in the face and if

WILL YOU LIKE ME IF …

you believe it's the right time to speak up, then say it. I'm not giving you permission to lay into someone you dislike greatly or to put others down. I'm encouraging you to speak up when it matters. To set boundaries with people who ask a lot of you. To say no when you're depleted. To speak your ideas out loud. I'm inviting you to do so whether you think you'll be liked or not.

Will You Like Me If... I'm a Big Success?

I pull the fader down on the radio desk in front of me and say goodbye to the listeners, one arm already in a coat sleeve. Sprinting up the stairs at Radio 1, I throw out cursory goodbyes to team members and Clare on reception. Hurling myself into a waiting cab, I sit back and catch my breath. The smell of the air freshener hanging from the windscreen instantly makes me feel queasy. I've drunk too much coffee. My body pulses with caffeine and cortisol.

Heathrow is a buzz of travellers dragging wheeled suitcases in zigzags. I fumble in my bag, past the tubes of lip gloss, packet of cigarettes, multiple note pads, and retrieve my passport. It's going to be tight. I am on time for my flight to Los Angeles, but the connecting flight after that to Las Vegas leaves no room for error. Even though it's a problem I don't need to consider for at least eleven hours, I can feel the anxiety kicking in.

The plane has a hushed quiet that feels like an instant antidote to the bustle of the airport. I go through my usual ritual when flying long haul alone. A gin and tonic, half a film and 5mg of melatonin. I manage to sleep a little, but I'm overtired and also know I need to be alert and ready to work when I land.

I look out of the window and see LA lit up like a Christmas tree below. It's evening on the west coast and as the wheels touch down on the tarmac, I calculate that I've been awake

WILL YOU LIKE ME IF ...

for twenty hours – and I've still got to fly to Las Vegas. My legs feel heavy as I sprint to the domestic departures terminal of LAX airport. My suitcase scrapes along the sidewalk behind me as I try and navigate my way through car parks and busy taxi ranks. The lady at the check-in desk looks at me sympathetically. 'We've just closed check-in. Sorry.' My heart sinks. I cannot miss this flight.

A figure looms behind me and I watch as the lady's face warms and brightens like the sun. 'It's your lucky day,' she says to me, pointing at a man in uniform behind me. Apparently, it's customary to allow members of the armed forces onto flights even after check-in has closed. I slip onto the plane with him, thanking the universe as I do so. It's 10.30pm when I land in Las Vegas, which means it's now 6am back home. I've officially been awake for 24 hours and I've not even started filming yet.

I dump my bags at the hotel and head out to meet the crew at Nobu. Paris Hilton, whom I'm making a documentary about, greets me warmly and hands me a shot of tequila. The punch of the alcohol burns my throat and makes me feel instantly intoxicated.

We film late into the evening. More tequila, a nightclub, a bowling alley in her room. By this point, I'm not sure what day it is. My body is craving sleep and breakfast simultaneously but my mind still registers nighttime. The weekend continues in a blur of a Kylie Minogue concert, meeting a member of Bros after his residency, another club, a roped-off area in

I'M A BIG SUCCESS?

a nightclub, flashbulbs on cameras, hugging a toilet seat because I've drunk too much.

Somehow, I'm now back at Las Vegas airport, walking around the food court with glazed eyes. I'm starving, hungover, sleep-deprived. I reach into my bag to pull out my wallet. I need sustenance. A blueberry muffin that is twice the size of the ones back home seems to grin at me from the glass cabinet in a coffee shop. My hand sweeps the inside of my bag, but there's no wallet. A hazy memory flashes up: throwing clothes into my suitcase only hours before, having not been to bed. My wallet is in my suitcase, which is now winging its way to the plane. For the first time in my life, I consider stealing. I need food or I might faint or vomit in the middle of the airport.

The first leg of the journey home is painful. The congealed egg I'm served makes me retch and I know it's not worth trying to sleep as the flight is so short. Luckily, I sleep a little on the way from Los Angeles to Heathrow and eat several bread rolls alongside my meal to soak up any residual alcohol.

I breathe in the cool morning air as I leave Heathrow. Birdsong titters around my ears as I look for a cab. It's Monday morning and I need to get to Radio 1 for my show at 10am. The weekend feels like a fever dream. Was there a goat in Paris Hilton's hotel room or did I dream that on the flight? I'll only know once I look back on the photos I've taken on my camera.

I walk back into the reception of Radio 1 only two days after my departure, yet I've lived a month in that time. My

WILL YOU LIKE ME IF ...

hands slightly shake as I push the fader back up to say good morning to the listeners. I'm all adrenalin. Another day begins that I will race through, which will lead to another that's the same, and another after that. On repeat. At twenty-seven years old, I believe I must keep climbing. Reaching for the stars. The only way is up. To the top, where the big success stories live. Where I will be liked by everyone. *How do I get there?* I wonder daily. By never, ever stopping.

I enjoy thinking back to this period of my life. I loved the adventure at the time – how utterly bonkers it all was. Back then, life was like one never-ending workday: I moved from one project to another without so much as breathing. I knew how lucky I was that all these opportunities were coming my way, and so, as I had no responsibilities other than my two cats, I worked every day that I could. I felt I had to be seen as successful by other people – that used to feel very important to me. I needed them to witness my hard work too; I didn't want succeeding to look effortless. I thought if they saw how much I was striving, they would see some value in me. And I thought a condition of being 'successful' was that I had to be filling every minute of the day, taking zero rest. I was on a constant exhausting push to some sort of career nirvana. *Once I arrived there, I would feel loved, respected, popular,* I thought. For years, I assumed that climbing to the top,

I'M A BIG SUCCESS?

planting my flag in the summit, would bring me some relief. Surely then I would feel loved and *good enough*.

But does that kind of pinnacle actually exist? Is there one single point for any of us, whatever we do or whatever our goals are, where if we reach it, we will feel like a success and all of the self-doubt will magically drop away? I think probably not. There is always going to be a bigger goal, a meatier challenge, a new height to reach. I'm not sure many people do ever feel successful. There is always another goal or someone doing better. I've interviewed countless successful people and there is nearly always insecurity and a desire to better themselves in some way.

Work did enable me to feel good about myself – but only in the sense that I created an equation that meant I could only feel OK if lots of other people liked me, and I assumed that the more people I won over, the better I would feel. This only further fuelled the inner voice telling me I needed to try harder, do better, work more. Pinning all of my self-esteem to work meant that I couldn't stop.

I can now see that a lot of these beliefs around success were also coming from a place of ego. For many years, I identified as a popular and in-demand broadcaster and my ego needed the reassurance of that being reflected back by others around me. The more others agreed with my ideas about who I was, the easier it felt to believe them. Other people's view of me as good at my job helped me to believe I deserved to be where I was. The trouble arrived when I believed that without that identity, I had no actual value. Because when you build up a framework like I had, using a load of external stuff to prop up your self-esteem without any inner work being done, things will always unravel.

How important is it to you that the outside world sees you as a success? Lots of us feel our work is a big part of who we are, and I think that's completely fine. But when you're being really honest with yourself, do you believe that without a certain level of success, you'll be less likeable? Less valued? Do you think people will like you more once you achieve a certain goal or hit a milestone? Of course, this might not be in your working life. This sort of thing can show up in how you believe others perceive you as a parent, a friend, a good citizen, a homemaker, or simply in how much you fit into a day.

Once you've deliberated that initial question, now ask yourself how important success is without any outside opinion. If you achieved something you wanted and there was no one there to see it – maybe you couldn't tell anyone for some reason – would it still feel good? How much of you thinks that you'll feel better, more worthy or more settled if there is a moment where that success is somehow 'completed'?

Being successful at something feels amazing. Of course it does. And we want to believe we can succeed, otherwise it's hard to bother in the first place. But the important lesson that I had to learn is that self-worth cannot come from outside validation. Many of us assume that validation from others will support our self-esteem, but only we can do that. If we

I'M A BIG SUCCESS?

don't believe we are good enough, we could have a football pitch full of people shouting about how great we are, but we will not hear it. I've chatted to actors who have felt depressed when walking a red carpet. Musicians who crumble when they come off stage. Business owners who don't feel they're worthy. It's easy to assume that famous people must feel great about themselves. Standing on a stage with a whole crowd howling your name and applauding must confirm that you deserve your success, right? In reality, I think many people who end up in the public eye do so because they crave a little extra outside adulation. Success may or may not make you more likeable, but on its own, it cannot make you like yourself.

At a point when, from the outside, I would have looked like I was having the most success, I was actually going through the most miserable period of my life. Depression usually brings some mates along for the ride, and mine dragged insecurity and paranoia along with it. I believed every terrible thing written about me, lapped up negative social media comments like a thirsty old dog, and would then spiral further. My confidence plummeted and left me in a pool of self-loathing. How could I be unhappy with a job like mine, earning money, with a roof over my head? I hated myself for not enjoying any of it and tried to bury the feelings further. I had pinned all of my hopes on the success I now had and it seemed to be letting me down. I felt foolish and tricked. Surely when you have dreams and work hard, and you achieve what you set out to, you should feel happy, elated, and like you deserve it ... right?

Why did I need to be loved by strangers? Why did I long for a bigger audience and more noise around me? I'm still trying to figure those answers out, but what I do know is that around this time, I quickly realised that being a big success would not save me. It wouldn't stop me from disliking myself and it wouldn't give me the confidence I was hoping for.

I've since interviewed countless people who have found themselves in a very similar hole. It's been referred to as rock bottom, ground zero, a dark patch, a nightmare. None of it sounds fun, but the thing I have in common with every one of these individuals is not just the huge low, but also the opportunity to redefine how you see the world and success. It is almost impossible not to: if you want out of the darkness and you desire change, you have to reconsider everything. So as much as I wouldn't want to repeat that chapter of my life, I can look back with gratitude. It forced me to re-evaluate my choices in life and what I believed I needed.

When I was pregnant with my second child, Honey, I started to address these ideas I had built up about myself and my career. I wondered what it would be like to leave my shiny radio job and therefore lose what had become a huge part of my identity. Would people see my departure as failure, or value me less? How would I feel without a job at a huge radio station propping up my self-worth? Although I was terrified about all of the above, I jumped out of the plane.

I'M A BIG SUCCESS?

I think pregnancy and early motherhood is a time when many women question their roles in the world anyway. You can feel like you are free falling away from everything you know. Your normal goes out of the window and along with it, sleep, a social life and sanity. After a sickly pregnancy that felt like I had food poisoning aboard a storm-battered boat for nine months, I relished looking after my newborn alongside Rex, who was a toddler at the time. Yet there was a niggling voice that told me that I was fading away. The outlines of my identity were being rubbed out like chalk from a blackboard. I started to wonder how I would reply to the questions, 'What are you up to at the moment?', 'What's in the pipeline?' or 'What do you do?' to people who didn't know who I was.

Slowly, over the years, I have created my own definition of success. The world often tells us what it looks like and subsequently should feel like. But I realised I needed to stop looking outside of myself for the answers and start playing by my own rules. Nearly a decade into my next chapter running *Happy Place*, I think I've managed to understand what success genuinely means for me. I am still in the public eye and I get a lot of great feedback about the podcast. But the difference is that this time it's on my terms. I am not doing it entirely for outside validation. When I do get it, it can still feel rather lovely, but I have to watch myself. I'm now more focused on whether or not I believe what I'm creating will be of use. Will it help someone, will it create positivity in the world rather than have a negative impact? That's what success feels like to me now.

I've learned that success isn't a box-ticking exercise or some sort of mad trolley dash of achievement – it's actually a moveable feast, with no set date, time or strong feeling attached to it. Success might be the sense of achievement you get from simply trying. Or the people you meet along the way. Or what you learned from the experience. The 'success' might take years, or you might change your mind about what that looks like, or it might feel like you never quite reach it. When we land on this idea, we can perhaps see that success isn't the outcome at the end, a linear path to the top, but instead is made of sporadic, fleeting moments where we have felt aligned, connected or peaceful in our day. This one precious life we have isn't about becoming a success so those around us like us. Define success for yourself. Don't pin all your self-worth to one successful outcome.

Cab drivers, camera people I used to work with and sometimes complete strangers have on occasion said to me, 'God, I haven't seen you on TV for ages, what are you up to?', at which I flinched and felt punched in the gut. I wanted to shout, 'I'VE NEVER BEEN SO BUSY. I RUN A BUSINESS AND WORK EVERY BLOODY DAY.' The thought of them assuming I don't work made me full of outrage and frustration. But why? Why does it matter if someone I barely

I'M A BIG SUCCESS?

know or don't know at all thinks I'm lying about at home all day? What has it got to do with them?

I definitely used to use how busy I was as one marker of how successful I was. If I filled my days, my weeks, my evenings without ever pausing for breath, that must mean I am working hard and therefore doing well, right? I think a lot of us think like this at times, particularly women. We fill our time with tasks that have to be done, those that might need to be done, and those that probably do not need to be done at all. We conflate busyness with success and assume that if we are constantly on the go, we are succeeding. But how true is this?

Culturally, we are not good at allowing ourselves rest. We might see it as failure. Down time might scare us. We might have to stop and look at ourselves that bit more closely if we do. In 2024, I went to the doctors because the small lump I had been aware of for two years that sat on my jawline below my ear, seemed to have grown. After an ultrasound and biopsy, I was diagnosed with a benign tumour on my parotid (salivary) gland. When I had my tumour removal operation in December 2024, I found hospital to be almost a refuge. I say this wincing and with an apology, as of course many people find themselves in hospital for months, even years, wishing they could get back to their normal lives. But I want to be honest. It forced me to stop. It made me rest. The nurses kept asking if I wanted visitors or to leave my room for a short stroll up the corridor, but I didn't. I wanted to be in that room on my own, resting. I felt no guilt or failure in that room. I felt the exhaustion from years of pushing leak out of me. Nurses took care of me. Prior to that, I clearly subconsciously saw asking for help as defeat. *I must do it all on my own*, I thought. *That's real success.* Though I think I might now class that as straight-up martyrdom. But – what the hell? If going to hospital was the only way I was going to rest, then that had to be a wake-up call. Something must be off kilter.

Many of us are in the habit of pushing ourselves to breaking point. The definition of burnout is an all-encompassing exhaustion that's experienced mentally, physically and emotionally. There are varying factors that may lead you to burnout and one of them is people pleasing. When you prioritise other people's needs, desires and opinions over your own, you're going to deplete yourself in every way. Not letting yourself pause or rest, filling your time to try to show how successful you can be in all areas, will at some point lead you down this road unless radical rest is imposed.

Radical rest is almost an art form: the intersection where self-compassion meets surrender. Confidence needs to be in place to stick to your guns, set boundaries and not care what others think of your rest. It might mean cancelling plans or asking your parents or mates to look after your kids for the day. It might mean changing how you work, and could force you to ask questions about how much you prioritise your health and welfare.

If, like I had, you have forgotten how to rest, have a think

I'M A BIG SUCCESS?

about what brings you ultimate comfort. I now know that I like solitude and a hot bath with a good book. It's that simple. Ensuring I have one moment on my own in the bath a week is not self-indulgent, it is essential. It doesn't always happen, but I try and give myself that time each week. Sometimes when I slip into the tub, I hear a voice in my head – *Ohhh, what would other people think about you having a bath at 2pm on a Tuesday? This isn't how successful people live their lives. Lying in the bath, how bloody lazy.* Yet I know after its yabbering protest, it'll peter out and I'll let myself enjoy every bloody minute. What does rest look like to you? If you're not quite sure, have fun experimenting.

I'm also less bothered about filling every second of my day to prove to myself and others that I am worthy. Some weeks will be insanely busy, and I will be chasing my tail. That is usually the nature of solo parenting and having a job. But I'm not forcing myself through an inhumane list of tasks, hoping to feel some level of worthiness by the end of it. I'm not waiting for someone to say, 'Oh my God, HOW do you do it?' A successful day is now one where I know I've worked more intuitively and honoured my own energy levels. Recently, in the middle of an insane week, I cancelled a meeting. Years ago, I would have pushed through and taken the meeting. I would have felt wretched at the end of a long day and the meeting would not have been productive, and yet the old me still would have seen the pushing through as the honourable option, the right thing to do. The old me would not have cancelled so as not to let anyone down. But the me of today, who knows her limits, said I couldn't do the meeting, even though it may have put others out.

Perhaps some of this redefining comes with age. I have a strong work ethic, and have cultivated it ever since I landed my first job as a teenager. I no longer need to prove to myself that I'm capable – I simply know I am. Luckily, I also have a lot of energy and am a grafter. Equally, I no longer need to prove to others that I work hard. The evidence is there (for me) to see, and I don't care if anyone else doesn't realise it.

So instead of going to that meeting, I got home from an already long day of podcast and radio recording and had a bath before my kids got in from school. My body sunk into the water as if it was sighing with relief. I had more energy for my children and didn't feel resentful that I hadn't had a break all day. That felt like a successful day.

The flipside of a lot of this is, of course, the fear of failure. What that means to us is subjective and usually quite personal, but I think in most of us, there lies an inbuilt subconscious fear that if we fail, we will be judged by others. It's often why we don't try in the first place. But failure, and things not panning out as we had hoped, is all part of the ride. There is no way to totally avoid it, unless you lock yourself away from all humans and opportunities until your time is up. At some point, we will all fail in our jobs, friendships, relationships, parenting. We know that this is part and parcel of being

I'M A BIG SUCCESS?

a human, yet we still lump pressure onto ourselves to be nailing it in all areas at once. We expect so much of ourselves. *Do not fail*, we tell ourselves throughout the day. *Don't mess up on the kids' homework, don't say something weird in that irrelevant interaction with the mum you don't really know on the school run, don't fail in your relationship, do all the things a wife/partner is supposed to do, don't fuck up at work even though you're hanging-out-your-arse tired.*

I've not met a single successful person who hasn't royally fucked up at some point. It's inevitable if we want to try something new. Every businessperson I've interviewed on *Happy Place* has had thirty ideas fail before they made traction. Every successful actor has felt the sting of rejection time and time again. Every thought leader or speaker has messed up on stage and said something incorrect or utterly weird. When we fail, we have a choice: to let it engulf us entirely or to see it for what it is – a moment of fallibility – and then pick ourselves back up.

I believe that putting so much effort into avoiding failure leads, once again, to burnout. When we expect success in every moment of our day, our week, our lives and don't let ourselves off the hook, we become exhausted. Our need to be seen as successful or nailing it at all times does not make us more likeable, as we subconsciously hope, but instead drains us of all energy.

Failure can also lead to a feeling of humiliation. When we fail in front of others, it hurts. Whether you lose your job

WILL YOU LIKE ME IF …

and your peers find out, your marriage ends and you feel lost, rejected or judged, or you try something new and tell your friends about it and it doesn't work out, it can be difficult to stay strong. When I have fluffed my lines on live TV, said something stupid or regrettable, or simply gotten it wrong, things can get noisy. And here comes one of the most valuable lessons in the book: things can get noisy with other people's opinions. There may be those who judge you, even those who vehemently dislike you, but you'll be OK as long as you don't turn on yourself. Read it again. You'll be OK as long as you don't turn on yourself.

What I mean by this is: as long as you don't start believing all the negativity and talking shit about yourself, then you will be OK. You will ride it out. You will stay true to yourself, even when it doesn't feel great. This thought alone has saved me in moments of utter despair when other people are gossiping about me or shouting about how awful/wrong/disliked I am.

Having your own back is imperative in noisy times. When the thunder is clapping and the skies are growing blacker, you mustn't turn the gun on yourself. And I say this from great experience. I abandoned myself for large portions of my thirties. I heard the outside noise, let the voices into my head and chose to walk away from ME. Bye, see ya later. Yup, not dealing with that today, thanks. I walked. And it hurt. I assumed that disliking myself would save me from feeling the gut punch of others not liking me.

It doesn't quite work like that, though, does it? I'm in the

I'M A BIG SUCCESS?

process of recovering a fully restored version of myself – but one that is full of chinks, bruises and cracks in the armour. I want to welcome back the past versions of me that did get it wrong, that did mess up, that did say something stupid, that massively failed. I don't want to leave those parts behind.

When did you go wrong? It could be a major life event or something small that niggles away at you. Did you abandon yourself? Did you let others make up the end of the story? Or did you stand by yourself with self-compassion and love? If you managed self-compassion, hats off – you're amazing. If you didn't, do not worry. It's never too late to welcome old parts of you back in.

Rejecting yourself is perhaps the worst kind of rejection. But it's not impossible to reverse the impact of those tricky times. It helps if you can find a photo from that era of your life. Even if that photo makes you cringe or repulses you, keep it nearby. Tell that version of yourself that you've got their back. You're there for them. It might feel excruciating at first but over time, it'll become easier and less trying.

Recently, I was going to dinner with someone who is very smart and impressive, and has enjoyed a long, successful career. I mentioned to my therapist that I was feeling particularly nervous in case I reverted back to the fifteen-year-old version of myself, who I deem to be a little bit silly, uneducated and annoying. I didn't want that part of me to show up, as I assumed my dinner companion would dislike it. My therapist suggested that I allow that version of myself to the table instead of entirely banishing her. Not to take over the show, but to sit nearby me (in an imagined sense) and for the forty-four-year-old, present-day version of myself to soothe her and let her know that she is welcome to the table. It's actually the fifteen-year-old me who I have to thank for getting my career started in the first place. She took the big step to follow big dreams, and was courageous and perhaps naive enough to believe she had what it takes. If anything, I should have her there as my esteemed guest, one that I'm incredibly grateful for.

Those who love you will not judge you if you fail. Those that do judge you are either too scared to try themselves or not worth listening to. I've failed over and over in all areas of my life and I've discovered that people really like it when you tell them about the times you didn't achieve what you set out to. They feel less ashamed about their own mistakes and appreciate your vulnerability. My own experience of this seems to be backed up by University of Pennsylvania psychology lecturer Angela Duckworth's studies on failure. During her failure research, she found that both individuals sharing moments of failure benefit. The one sharing feels more motivated after admitting to their failure, and the beneficiary feels less alone in their own failures. So, in fact, failing makes you that bit more likeable.

So let me wrap things up by asking you – what are you too scared to try because you fear failure and outside judgement? It's never just about failing at something; it's about

I'M A BIG SUCCESS?

the outside noise that may ensue. *What will people say if it goes wrong? Will people still like me if my idea flops? Will I be a laughingstock if I don't succeed?* We have no control over any of the outcomes, but none of these fears should stop us trying in the first place. So, what is it? What are you not doing because of this fear? Maybe you know instantly or perhaps you need to dig around for a bit and work out what you really want. Don't fixate on success – just focus on the thing you really want to do or try, knowing that outside opinion shouldn't be a deciding factor in whether you do or don't. Fuck outside opinion, and do it anyway.

There simply are no guarantees. Give things a go. Fail knowing that you tried. Judge others less and you'll care less when you yourself are judged. You'll understand the pain those finger-pointing types are in. Know that whether you succeed, fail or end up somewhere in between, you are still simply brilliant.

Will You Like Me If ... I Tame Myself?

As I sink my swollen body into the pool, I sigh heavily. The purple balloon that I've been told to imagine when I inhale seems to be at bursting point in my mind's eye. As I exhale, it feels as if my body may explode or I may gradually be torn apart into tiny fragments.

Another wave of intensity passes and I rest my head on my arm that's stretched out across the lip of the pool. I can hear the gentle tones of Holly, a hypno-birthing expert whose meditations I've become reliant on. As her voice leaves the nearby speaker and her whispers remind me to relax my abdomen, I feel safe. Her voice is incredibly familiar to me from listening to this exact meditation on repeat for months in the lead-up to today. Three hours pass by in a blur of deep inhales, long exhales, my back arching, my eyes closing.

Without warning, I flip onto my knees. I didn't know I was going to do it. It feels as if an ancient instinct has kicked in, one that generations of women have passed down in their cells to me. My body knows exactly what to do without my mind interfering at all. My arms are draped over the edge of the pool as I let my belly hang into the water. The intensity builds and I picture the big purple balloon filling with air. I imagine the muscles around my belly relaxing and a ripple of calm coursing through me. I've never been more focused in my life.

WILL YOU LIKE ME IF ...

In vast contrast to the laser-point focus is the wild noise that comes out of my mouth. It's uninhibited, loud, a lion's roar. I've never made a sound like it before. It's from the depths of me, but also seems to span back to my ancestors. It's not from the throat, but from my gut, my heart, my soul. My body moves in the freest way possible. An animalistic dance where I'm part feline, with roots grounding me to the earth, yet simultaneously high in the clouds. I'm volcanic, with each eruption silencing those nearby. They stand and watch and know that at this point, it's down to me and the baby. Teamwork in the truest sense.

I'd always been intrigued by the notion of pushing a baby out. When I had my first, I was administered an epidural and felt nothing at all as I strained and pushed. At times, I wasn't sure if my emulation of what I had seen actors do in movies was working at all. But this time, I'm drug-free, my body submerged in warm water, and I can feel the baby moving down. I'm not pushing at all. This tiny human who is about to make their entrance is tunnelling down, being pulled by nature and the cycle of life. I've never felt anything like it. I'm every season rolled into one. My pumping heart is as warm as the sun, my mind as quiet as a still winter morning, my inhibitions dropping like autumn leaves, all while new life is getting ready to blossom.

Normally, I hate making a scene. I may not come across as a deeply shy person, but I really don't like creating drama. Confrontation never sits easily with me and I don't like

I TAME MYSELF?

putting other people out. Of course, I have done all of those things many times over the years, but it's never with any sense of desire, comfort or often even consciousness. Usually, I like to suss out my surroundings to ascertain whether it's safe to make noise. If I'm with people I trust, I will chat relentlessly, laugh, get excitable and create a little fizz in the air, but with people I don't know – well, I prefer to stay quiet until I know it's OK to express myself. This safety catch seems to be massively absent as I undulate my spine in the water and release animal sounds. I do not care. I don't care if I'm being too loud for other labouring mums in the hospital. I don't care if the midwife thinks I'm being too much. I don't care if they'll talk about it later. I have very few thoughts at all. I feel raw and liberated and completely wild.

Even after I've given birth to my beautiful ginger queen Honey, I don't feel the urgent need to apologise, awkwardly laugh about it or explain myself. I'm still buzzing in the hum of the physical release and freedom. It's as if every cell in my body is vibrating. I'm the most alive I've ever been.

How often do you feel wild and completely free? I can count on one hand the times I have felt this way. Normally, I don't want to come across as too loud or brash, so I tame myself from natural excitement, rage or surprise. I'm perhaps scared of my natural propensity to feel a hell of a lot, so choose to actively numb myself so I react less. I don't want to be loud and unlikeable. I don't want to be brash and overreactive and push people away. So I tame my natural enthusiasm, as well as my anger. We subconsciously tame ourselves as we move through our days. In childhood, we shriek when excited, shout when we are frustrated, dance wildly when we feel the urge to move our bodies, laugh loudly without care, until that wildness and freedom gets bashed out of us as we become teenagers, then young adults. In adult life, we might tame ourselves by toning ourselves down. We may attempt to be more palatable by suppressing certain emotions we deem too big. We may cap our potential because we don't want to be seen as too show-offy or extra. We may push down tears and dull our enthusiasm so as not to rock the boat. We keep the straitjacket on to keep the peace. But don't you think it feels a little too tight, a bit too restrictive? A bit bloody exhausting yet boring at the same time? Wanna break free? I do!

Anger is perhaps seen as the pinnacle of wildness. There is no place for an angry woman. She is seen as wayward and mostly out of control. Men have for centuries had outlets for their anger, whether it's fighting in the street, chanting at football matches, pumping weights in the gym or playing contact sport. It is not only acceptable for a man to display anger, it's often celebrated and sometimes seen as strength. But an angry woman is seen as deranged, a drama queen, a psychopath, unhinged. And so the inevitable lava of rage

I TAME MYSELF?

fills our bodies, our hearts racing, and we don't know how to move through it.

When Oasis had their 2025 live tour, I went to see them at Wembley Stadium. Liam Gallagher was a wondrous tosser throughout: brash, regularly pissed off at the audience, ordering us to turn around or cheer fucking louder. His face and body language were combative and full of attitude. Whether it's how he really felt or all an act as part of his showman tendencies, no one questioned it. My friends and I laughed as he called us all mad heads; the crowd roared when he angrily pointed at someone in the audience. I wonder what the reaction would have been if the lead singer was female. I can easily imagine a *Daily Mail* headline boiling with outrage and condemnation.

Anger is perhaps the emotion we try most urgently to tame to remain likeable. Yet feeling anger is healthy; we just need some guidance on what to do with it. We may assume the only way to rid ourselves of it is to pass it on to someone else. To shout at the idiot in your life who is pissing you off. To rage at others about how awful that thing that happened to you was. To send abusive texts to the person who will not listen to you. I have done all of those things and I know they don't work. I'm left feeling utterly dreadful and usually sink into self-loathing. More recently, I have been adopting other methods and am reaping the benefits.

The opposite of shouting at someone who is making you rage is not suppressing it altogether. It's to really let yourself feel it and then decide how you might want to get it out of your body. When we store anger in the body without an outlet, it can make us very sick. I've explained why I believe the tumour I had on my salivary gland in 2024 was a little to do with the resentment and anger I had been feeling throughout a lot of my adult life. Anger that I couldn't (wouldn't) speak aloud or process. Anger that others treated me badly (a lot of the time, I let them). Anger that there had been moments of pure injustice without a positive conclusion. It was all sat in my clenched jawline, growing like a little ball of fire. It's impossible to suppress any emotion forever, and anger really doesn't like to be silenced. You can try to push it down and cover it with a willing smile so you remain likeable, but it'll always come out in the end – either in an eruption or in a quiet but steady overflowing of your very full cup, after which it seeps into multiple areas of your life.

Think of the last time you were really pissed off, but didn't say anything or act on the anger because you didn't want to rock the boat. It's more than likely that at some point that day or week, when you were trying to box in the emotion and keep a lid on it, something small tipped you over the edge. You stubbed your toe, someone cut you off in traffic, your kid spilled a glass of juice everywhere. One small mishap and that suppressed anger about something entirely different comes raging to the surface. If we can all learn to embrace the unruliness of anger and channel it in healthy ways, the rest of our life becomes that much easier.

I TAME MYSELF?

Suppressed anger can also show up as anxiety. The panic attacks I had for years were mainly due to anger I had pushed down so deep I didn't even know it was there. Early in my weekly therapy sessions, my therapist suggested that I didn't have panic disorder, as I had feared, but I actually wasn't looking at the anger I was feeling. I wasn't allowing myself to acknowledge it at all. I didn't identify as an angry person – which, looking back, is mad as I was fucking fuming inside. Anger felt too dangerous to engage with. If I looked at it, I would have to make changes, to tell people no, and then they would hate me. I wouldn't be seen as a good person with a moral compass, strong values, an understanding of rules, composure. You know, all the things a good girl is. So instead, I was wracked with anxiety and often felt exhausted.

For almost a year, I worked with my therapist on taking the anger seriously rather than making excuses and pretending it wasn't there. Then it was time to pinpoint why I was angry and to look at whether I had more autonomy in certain situations than I believed I had. Taking the anger seriously gave me the opportunity to look at the scenarios in my life that I thought were trapping me. I was able to question the beliefs I had about who I was and the world around me, what I deserved and what I was allowed to do. Many of the subsequent realisations I had meant I was confronted with the trappings of being a good girl. I must stay in line, do as I'm told, not piss anyone off. Yet the payoff of remaining a good girl was too big.

My therapist has, on so many occasions, reminded me to treat my emotions with the gravity they deserve. She'll stop me mid rant and say, 'OK, let's take that seriously.' She can see I'm about to spin off course and either move away from the subject of anger or explain why I shouldn't really be angry at all. Prioritising our emotions is incredibly important. Anger feels scary to take seriously because it can appear to be very out of control. It doesn't have neat lines or borders and you're never quite sure where it's going. Yet it's also fucking powerful. When we channel it with authority, we can change our lives and other people's positively.

I have danced around the edges of these changes; I'm still nervous to let other people witness my anger. I'm not 100 per cent comfortable with it, so assume others won't be either. But I've had small victories where I've used anger to move my body with meaning, create new boundaries that feel healthy and passionately move forward through some pretty challenging times.

If you are scared of your inner anger, just know that many other women feel exactly the same. We have been told for centuries that our rage is not acceptable, so we've let it curl up into a flaming ball that sits in the pits of our stomachs, like it did in those who came before us. A good way to start to unleash that wild power is through physical movement. For years, I was very shut off physically. I never understood the yoga teacher's instruction to feel into my hips, or sense what was tense in my body. One bit of homework from a teacher

I TAME MYSELF?

I was working with was for me to really sit and notice what my body feels like throughout the day. Are my shoulders tight, is my tummy tense, are my neck muscles in contraction? Now that I can feel my body, I know where the anger and tension lives.

One of my favourite ways to move anger on is to shake. Animals do it in the wild after they've experienced trauma. We humans have forgotten how to do it. I stand in my kitchen with my arms above my head, shaking manically. I let every bit of skin, fat and muscle shake away from the bone and tissue. I let my head roll, my torso loosen and soften. I often holler, shout or wail at the same time. Sometimes I let myself shout all the expletives. If someone in my life has pissed me off, I'll shout about how angry I am and call them every name under the sun in my empty kitchen. I've said what is needed, but nobody has been hurt in the process. I've got the words out of me and released the anger from my body. At first, I felt mortified doing this, even when on my own. I was embarrassed for myself even without spectators. Now, I don't give a shit. I let myself be wild, untamed and loud. I move the energy through my body and concentrate on my throat and jaw, where I know a lot of my anger has been stored before. Trapped words, frustrations, the feeling of being unable to stand up for myself when people were collectively talking shit about me. I have to really exorcise those demons.

So try it. Stand in a quiet spot in your house and let rip. Push through the cringe and alien feeling of being completely uninhibited. Make noise and move your body. You can also healthily rid your body of anger by running, boxing, dancing, singing loudly. Whatever it is that gives you a feeling like you are moving through it. You may still cognitively feel pissed off with someone or something. Your irritating work colleague isn't going to miraculously stop moaning just because you shook your limbs that morning, but you won't be holding your resentment in your body. Therapy, talking to people who love you and you trust, and doing more of what lights you up can help the mental side of built-up anger. Remember: when used properly, anger is power.

When I picture an untamed, wild woman, I see a silhouette moving freely, arms outstretched wide, head swinging from side to side, bare feet stomping on the ground. Dancing is pure liberation. I love nothing more than letting go on the dance floor. A wedding is my flavour of choice. Give me a disco ball, the cheesiest music possible and the opportunity to take my shoes off and I'm happy. But for a long time, I saw letting go and having fun as extremely dangerous. The fear was almost subconscious, but the signs were all there. I turned down almost all social invitations and if I did manage to get myself out of the house in the evening, I would be planning my exit strategy before I had even arrived. On the rare occasions I drank, I would start to panic when the feeling of intoxication kicked in. The edges blurring, the inhibitions loosening. I would feel untethered and worried something bad might happen. The wildness that sat beneath the surface

I TAME MYSELF?

scared me shitless. What was that version of me capable of? What might she say in that state? What decisions would she make? If I truly let go, danced freely, spoke without overthinking every word, moved as if I loved my body, what would others think? Would they find my wild side as scary as I did? Would they think I was a show-off, cocky, too much? I tamed myself to avoid the possibility of being unlikeable. I think this also came from a belief that loosening my grip on the reins meant I was a terrible person, a woman with no self-control or morals. Intellectually, I know this isn't true, but the fear steered me towards the safety of home time and time again. I now wonder how much fun I missed out on.

More recently, I've pushed myself to go out and let loose and – spoiler alert – nothing bad has happened. I wasn't punished by the gods for having fun. There was no retribution the following day. What I believe I was truly scared of was being free. It was the unknown. The familiar was being in control, keeping my unruliness locked away, the mess stuffed in cupboards, with polite, considered chit-chat and an adherence to etiquette that kept me smiling and nodding. That felt safe. No one could get me or judge me. I would have preferred people to feel indifferent about me rather than dislike me.

These days, I'm not as definite about that. I wouldn't go as far as to say that I don't care at all if people dislike me altogether, but I also know I really don't want to dilute myself. Dita Von Teese recently said on my podcast that 'only mediocrity is safe from ridicule'. I don't want to be mediocre.

WILL YOU LIKE ME IF ...

I have never felt comfortable being average at anything. I would rather be bloody dreadful but have tried or worked hard to be excellent at something. The middle ground bores me senseless. So why did I allow myself to sink into the safe yet dull arms of mediocrity for so long? As I creep towards the middle of my forties, it's time to have some fucking fun.

In the dictionary underneath the word 'wild', it states: '(an animal or plant) living or growing in the natural environment, not domesticated or cultivated'. The word 'growing' jumps out at me here. When we are truly, wildly ourselves, we grow. We push our own boundaries, make mistakes, trip up, learn and grow. When we cap and limit ourselves due to fear, we stop learning and growing. Making big decisions can seem utterly wild and always involves risk. Whether we take the new path or not is purely down to mindset. Yes, there might be more barriers in place for some of us than others, but the main difference between people who take risks and ones who don't is all in the mind.

For various reasons, some people are just better able to sidestep the fear of what others will say. For them, failing does not determine the entirety of their self-worth and outside commentary is merely a distraction. I've been pretty good at taking outrageous risks over the years, but I've also found the outside noise incredibly hard to stomach. Making changes that affect others is burdensome and can derail you if you're not willing to completely back yourself up.

The front cover of this book shows a glorious gold middle

I TAME MYSELF?

finger swinging from a necklace. I immediately loved the idea, but then a secondary voice entered the scene. *What if people think you're outrageous and scandalous for choosing such a punchy front cover? What if they think you're rude or too provocative for choosing such a bold statement to represent your book?* The good girl option would be something more palatable, cute and inoffensive. Luckily, I was able to override that niggling voice and go with the option that felt most authentic to me, irrespective of the imagined opinions of others. The middle finger is pointing at people pleasing. It's a sign for us all to give people pleasing the middle finger. Rather than seeing this choice as unsavoury, I see it as pure liberation. How often do you make decisions based on what everybody else wants? How often do you park wild ideas? How often do you stay put because you're scared of what a new chapter might look like and what others will say? How scared are you of the uninhabited, untamed, honest version of yourself that lurks within? This front cover is very much the wilder side of me saying hi.

One way to get to know that part of yourself is to get a pen and some paper and write freely. If you want to, you can burn this piece of paper afterwards so that it belongs to you and you only. When you touch pen to paper, start by writing, 'What I really want is ...' Then see what comes out. Do you want to leave your job, get a tattoo, have better sex, start art classes, have more time to yourself, start wearing hats, say what you've deemed to be unsayable, scream loudly in the woods? Writing it all down doesn't mean you have to instantly action it, but it will give you clarity on what's lurking beneath the confines of being the person everybody else needs you to be. You can always start small, ticking one thing off the list that feels the safest. A litmus test for what could be. Big changes take time. There is no rush with any of it.

Each time we try something new, we prove to ourselves that it's safe to step out of the good-girl straitjacket. Even if others have something to say about your decision/new path/new hat, it's a chance to practise doing it regardless of their opinions. Let others have their say, then do it anyway.

So much of the fear comes from our early lives. Maybe we still feel scared we are going to be told off. I have had so many conversations with adults about how any form of confrontation makes them feel as if they're about to be put on the naughty step. I get it. If you were told as a child to shut up, or reprimanded for doing something someone else deemed outlandish, then you may well find it incredibly difficult to rebel against the norm. What we learn in childhood informs such a large part of how we see the world as adults. I remember someone calling me a 'big mouth' when I was about twelve years old. That comment lives rent-free in my head and often echoes in my mind when I feel myself getting carried away. When drunk and loose-lipped, or caught in a vortex of gossip or over excitement, I can feel the sting of that comment all over again. As an adult, I can now rationalise the comment and know it was throw-away and directed at a kid who was

I TAME MYSELF?

a little loud and excitable. I don't need to lug it around at age forty-four. But it's hard to lose the label mentally. That one comment alone has tamed me in so many situations. It has zipped me up, taped my mouth and made me self-loathe when I feel I've stepped over the line.

Can you determine which comments thrown around in your past have stuck? Again, grab a pen and paper and write them all down. Do they need to remain in your psyche, informing how you move through your life? Can you challenge any of them and get curious about what sits beneath that self-imposed limitation? What part of yourself are you scared to show others? Which bits of your unique personality are you worried others will reject?

There is a beautifully free and feral version of YOU waiting to be unveiled. That version of you may be buried beneath years of parenting, social conditioning, knockbacks and losing yourself, but it's in there. Remember, we've been collectively conditioned to find dynamic, uninhibited women utterly terrifying, but that doesn't mean you shouldn't be one. Wild women are dangerous because they are fucking powerful. Witches were hanged and burned at the stake from the 1400s to the 1700s. Women who broke free from societal norms, like the suffragettes, were condemned and punished. Women in modern culture who have shown up as their true uninhibited selves have been viewed as outliers. Malala Yousafzai, who from the age of eleven stood up for her rights to education, was shot in the head for speaking out.

WILL YOU LIKE ME IF ...

She has continued to be shouted down by some for her beliefs and even called a porn star on social media for daring to break Pashtun tradition by wearing jeans. Serena and Venus Williams, who have dominated a sport that was up until they came along predominantly white. Both sisters say they have been treated much more harshly than their male counterparts when they've demonstrated emotional outbursts on the tennis court. Both stand up for gender and racial equality. Then there's Karren Brady, who after becoming football team Birmingham City's managing director, received a devastating amount of sexism and abuse. I could fill a book with brilliant women who have broken through barriers and been shouted down because of it. The patriarchy has rejected women like that because it undermines the infrastructure we are so very used to. It is not easy to be unconventional and boundary pushing, but we need more women showing up authentically and more women harnessing their true power. We can all see how a world run by men isn't working out that well, right? We need to understand how much strength and fire in our bellies we all have and start using it.

That burning fire will look different for each one of us, so spend a little time getting curious as to what that means to you. Being truly yourself without inhibition doesn't mean life will immediately get easier; if anything, it'll initially become more challenging. But in the long run, it's so much better for you and everyone around you. It doesn't matter if you're still scared and fear what everyone thinks, but it does matter

I TAME MYSELF?

if you relent and tame yourself further. Living authentically doesn't mean without fear. To live fearlessly is a big ask. It's human nature to feel nervous about outside opinion and consequences – what counts is how much you let it hinder you. The sweet spot is living alongside the fear, but viewing it with curiosity and putting it in its place where necessary. It can have a place at the table as long as it's not taming you.

Will You Like Me If ... I Give You Everything?

I emerge from the general anaesthetic and my first thought is *Why am I crying?* I literally wake up mid cry. The tears are salty droplets of relief and gratitude. There is an absolute clarity as to what is important in my life. Amongst the tears is the awareness that this reaction is a total cliché. Fuck, couldn't I have been more original post-surgery?

I cry as I'm wheeled on the bed into the lift as the rest of the world around me slowly comes into focus. A nice nurse with red hair stands next to my horizontal body and smiles gently. More tears. If finding the tumour was a wake-up call, then this bit is where I'm properly awake. I'm present and listening. *Hello, universe, I get the message, now what?*

A month before, I had popped to the doctors because the little lump on my neck I had spent two years fiddling with when reading with my kids in bed had grown. At first to the size of a pea, then more recently to a large grape. As usual, I felt embarrassed that I was wasting the doctor's time, but he sent me for a scan anyway, just to be sure. I tiptoed into the scan feeling embarrassed all over again that things had gone this far. Hearing the word 'tumour' was a shock, but not a horrifying one. At this point, it was unclear as to whether it was benign or not, but the doctor felt it was more than likely not cancerous.

Even with uncertainty in the air, I felt a profound sense of calm. This was an alarm bell. One that had been lightly humming in the background for years. The fact it had just gotten a hell of a lot louder was almost a relief – now I couldn't ignore it. If I don't change my ways after this, then I'm an idiot. I need to stop saying yes to everyone and everything. It has to stop. I must keep something back for me. I must learn to say no. I must stop giving my whole self away. But how?

Now I'm lying in the hospital bed, nibbling on white toast with butter, my face numb yet simultaneously sore, wondering how I can change my life. How do I change my personality overnight? How do I just stop being a people pleaser and start saying no?

I turn my phone screen to my ear and take a photo of my face. An incision runs from the top of my ear down to the bottom, and then back up around the other side in a big loop. A small tube pokes from my neck. I had no idea it was there, but can now see it's collecting blood and pus, which then sits in a little accordion-shaped container that is strapped to my collarbone. Let this incision be a reminder of what needs to change. Let the scar that will follow constantly point me to make better decisions.

It's blindingly clear to me now that for a large portion of my life, I've been a grade-A people pleaser. I would give away all of my energy, time, words and resources to keep everyone happy – and to avoid my personal fear of being disliked.

I GIVE YOU EVERYTHING?

For years, I had been taking on responsibilities emotionally, practically and otherwise. When someone asked me for something, I said yes before they'd even finished their sentence. I should give, because I could. And I didn't want to rock the boat, so I kept doing everything that was asked of me, even when I had nothing left to give. Doing, helping, running, giving, handing over, organising. I was burned out regularly and resentful about many situations in my life. Being resentful is dangerous, as you're not owning up to your own part in the problem. When we point fingers or store up tension due to how much we are giving away, we are refusing to look in the mirror. We cannot control how other people behave, but we can very much change how we interact with the world around us.

I was holding the door wide open, letting anyone in to take what they wanted. But rather than simply shutting the door, I would feel rage pulsing through me and would sit in a puddle of resentment. I'm now in a place where I feel entirely accountable for the resentment I felt. I'm not here to blame anyone. I was giving too much of myself to literally everyone I knew. How were they to know I was expelling the same amount of energy to multiple people? They couldn't possibly. I left no time for myself, didn't give myself permission to rest ever, and would crawl into bed most nights feeling utterly wrecked. Maybe I was pleasing the majority of people by doing so. Maybe they liked me because I was giving them my all. But the cost was too big.

WILL YOU LIKE ME IF ...

The constant need to give must have started in childhood, or at the very latest in my teens. I can see how I have always had a very responsible side. One who wants to take care of everyone and makes sure I'm doing my bit. Earning money from my mid teens was liberating but came with responsibility. To not piss it up the wall, to help those who needed it, to always give because I was one of the lucky ones. And I was lucky. I still am. I'm always grateful that I earn money for doing a job I mostly love, but over the years, I started to use this notion to punish myself. *You're too lucky*, I would tell myself. *Give more of your time, energy, resources away.* However, there's a fine line between giving and feeling the beautiful reverberations of that, and giving to the point of depletion. Previously, I had no grasp of this concept at all.

We can deplete ourselves in a plethora of ways. Energetically, financially, emotionally, practically. We give and we give, and don't take the time to check the gauge to see how much we have left in the tank. If we were cars, we would be stranded somewhere on the hard shoulder of the M1 because we didn't look at the dashboard. To be able to offer someone help or a listening ear is a gift and may leave us feeling boosted, but when we are giving so much of ourselves to others mainly because we are scared of outside judgement, then the balance has tipped. So let's look at why that happens.

If you are a woman reading this, I'm sure you have felt on many occasions that you are giving too much. We have historically been labelled nurturers, carers, loving, gentle, so feel

I GIVE YOU EVERYTHING?

we have to live up to these qualities. We might also feel bound by outdated duty and expectation. It can often feel like there is always another person who needs us or wants something from us. Some of this might be bound up in how women operate in friendships. For example, I'm not sure my brother has ever given one of his mates a birthday card in his life. I am not throwing any shade on dear Jamie Cotton here at all; for men, gestures like this are simply not the done thing, whereas many women would feel terrible if we didn't send our mate a card or buy her/him a gift. I'm not entirely sure how, or when in history, this started for women, but after a quick browse online, the only thing the internet came up with was that women care more about expressing love. Who knows if this is absolutely true, but the fact remains that we put ourselves under much more pressure when it comes to this sort of thing.

I recently had an interesting conversation with my friend Jamie Laing, who told me about a time when he and a bunch of male mates were on holiday together for one of their birthdays. Jamie took a chance and suggested that they go round in a circle and say something lovely about the friend who was celebrating his birthday. It was met with eyerolls and laughter, as the usual dynamic was one of piss-taking and jibing. He eventually convinced them, and it ended up being a very beautiful moment of connection. This story tells me that there are many differences between how men and women socialise. Often, men will use piss-taking or discussing a subject

WILL YOU LIKE ME IF ...

like football or politics as a framework for their friendship. This is, of course, a generalisation, but one I think is true for many, especially older men. In female friendship groups, we seemingly need a lot more depth and mutual support. We want to be helpful and drop everything when a friend is in need. We'll talk for hours to help find solutions to problems and always be on call if someone is going through something challenging. This is obviously a beautiful way to support your mates, but it also shows how women ask a lot of themselves in all areas. We want to not only be there emotionally for our family, but also for our friends. I think it means that in most situations, we have normalised caring for other people's needs above our own.

I'm not suggesting any of us stop caring for our friends, but I am asking us to evaluate whether we are putting the same amount of care and attention into our own wellbeing. Having just read Elizabeth Gilbert's incredible new book *All the Way to the River*, I have a brand-new understanding of, shall we say, over-helping. I used to see it as my duty to help others. I would go out of my way – I mean very out of my way – to help others. From reading Elizabeth's book, I now see my supposedly saintly endeavours as something else entirely. The urge to help others didn't come from a purely benevolent place. Some of it came from people pleasing, but beneath that sat lots of unworthiness. Not believing I deserved some of the luck and opportunity I had received led me to give so much of myself away. My time, energy and money. Elizabeth talks

I GIVE YOU EVERYTHING?

about moments where she would force herself into the life of someone she believed was in need, showering them with anything they wanted and needed. All sounds gorgeous, right? Well, not entirely: often, when we do this, we don't ask the other person's full permission. We make assumptions about what they need and lump our generosity on them. I found these stories incredibly confronting – I could recognise multiple times in my life where I had tried to save someone, whether they wanted me to or not. Not only is that type of help slightly lacking true care and empathy, but it could also be potentially hindering that person from learning some big life lessons. This is the part of Elizabeth's book that had me sat upright with wide eyes. Wow, maybe I had meddled with someone else's life story whilst trying to save them. Perhaps they needed to hit rock bottom. Maybe they needed to feel all their feelings without my unlimited soothing. What a wake-up call. People pleasing and giving so much of myself away could actually be damaging in some way – and not just to me. What an amazing new perspective.

Motherhood is all about giving and even though we've (usually) made a choice to have a child, it doesn't mean we can't feel and acknowledge how much we are constantly giving, and subsequently find it very hard. Even if we have a forward-thinking partner in a heterosexual partnership, it is more than likely that we are still carrying the lion's share of the child-rearing duties, housework and emotional burden that come with being a mother and partner. This may seem like a huge generalisation, but it's one that holds. I've done a survey (texted my mates) and not one of them disagrees. We want women to go out and be the female boss and take over the world, but she better unload the bloody dishwasher whilst she's at it. She better not have forgotten that it's non-uniform day on Friday and the kid has to take in £2 cash for charity. It's not even so much the doing, though there is loads to do – it's the remembering and checking in and planning ahead and logistics and making sure you don't run out of loo roll. There is always one more person/pet that needs our attention or for us to do something for them. There is no time or space to say, 'I have nothing left. I'm on the floor.'

If you're a woman reading this and you don't feel pulled from pillar to post by other humans, then I commend you. Please can you write the sequel to this book about how you have achieved such a feat? Can it be called *Unavailable* or perhaps *Sorry, No, I Can't, Go Away*? Whatever you call it, I'll read it.

The caretaking onus has been heavy on women for many centuries, but there are singular challenges facing women in midlife today. Some of us find ourselves looking after young children and ageing parents at the same time. So much so, that there is now a term for it: the sandwich generation. It's become a hot topic because parents are living longer and women are having children later, on the whole, so a generation has found themselves squeezed between, running from dirty nappies to vulnerable elderly health issues. We are yet to find

I GIVE YOU EVERYTHING?

a social solution that takes the pressure of this stressful sandwich and are simply hoping that one human has the capacity to deal with it all on their own. If you're in that predicament currently, I really feel for you. No amount of positive mantras is going to feel helpful. It simply is a lot.

If you're living in this situation, or any similar one where you are dealing with something major that needs a lot of your attention, this is where it's crucial that people-pleasing ways stop. This is when you might feel absolutely OK saying no to helping at the school fair or taking your neighbour's dog for the weekend. You are simply under too much pressure already. If that person is pissed off, let them be. Move yourself higher up the ladder of priorities. The truth is that people are wrapped up in their own lives and may not have considered what's going on with you before they made their request, or they might not know about the pressures you are under. This can be annoying, but it also means you don't really have to consider them when you say no, beyond the usual politeness. There is always someone else who can run the tombola or dog sit. We can get into the mentality that it is always on us, because so much stuff at home realistically is – but it's not. That last part goes for all of us, not just those of us stuck in a stressful responsibility sandwich.

If we are going to avoid taking on everything to the point of burnout, we are going to have to be honest with ourselves. Even though some of our giving is rooted in duty, care and a sense of how we want to show up as a mother/wife/sister/

friend, some of our drive to continue giving so much of ourselves is rooted in the terror of others not liking us. We don't want to rock the boat, cause a stir, or have others bitching about us. So we give and give and give. We hand over our time like it won't run out one day. We say yes when we are screaming no inside. We buy gifts for other people when we are tight for time and cash. We help others in challenging times whilst ignoring our own.

Noticing the motivation or feeling that lies behind how much of yourself you are giving away to others is necessary, as it allows more clarity on whether you should say yes or no when you're asked to do something. If you know that giving your time and energy to someone else is going to feel good, then do it. If you're going to be full of resentment ten minutes after saying yes, then the answer should perhaps be no.

If I'm completely honest with myself, and you, I can easily tip into being a martyr. Refusing help, insisting (through gritted teeth) that I will do it all myself and then trudging on begrudgingly. When I find myself practising martyrdom, I know it's mainly for the sake of how others perceive me rather than a genuine desire to do it all myself. In these moments, I need people to see how much I'm suffering for others and how much I'm giving to everyone around me. *Look at me*, my ego shouts, *I'm doing it all alone and it's so hard. I'm giving and giving and it's all too much. Please notice. Please see my suffering. Please feel a bit sorry for me. But whatever you do,* DO NOT HELP ME.

I GIVE YOU EVERYTHING?

When we slip into martyrdom, we want praise. We want to be liked for our efforts and seen as stoic and maybe even for others to feel guilty along the way. *Their efforts aren't as great as ours*, we tell ourselves. *I'm suffering more.* As we further yearn for praise and attention, it becomes the suffering Olympics. Our ego doesn't want us to get help because then the spell is broken. We can't moan anymore or bitch about how no one helps us. I know when I'm doing this and it doesn't feel great. Our martyrdom is a clumsy cry for help and attention, yet it's never satisfied. The only way to climb out of it is to notice that we are craving attention and praise and then ask for help. Humbling, maybe even slightly embarrassing, but a lot better than harbouring resentment when people don't help because they have no idea we need it (often because we have been insisting that we don't).

The reality is that sometimes you need to ask others for what you need. Fuck, I am bad at this one. I believe I have to do it all myself and that I don't deserve help and that the person I've asked will be upset with me or think of me badly. Yet there is only one outcome in this scenario: I give and give, and don't ask for help, or for my needs to be met, and then I become resentful. Resentment leads to stress, which leads to less resilience, negatively impacted physical health and unhappiness. Not a great outcome, really, is it?

What I have found is that people actually, on the whole, like being asked for help. It assures them that you trust them, value them and feel safe enough to ask. On the rare occasions

WILL YOU LIKE ME IF ...

I have asked for help, it's been met with either genuine gratitude and care, or else honesty, which I've appreciated. When someone has explained why they can't help out, it gives me confidence to do the same. So I see asking for help as win-win. It may still be deeply uncomfortable, but at least I've flipped the risk of rejection on its head enough to be able to stand it.

As well as giving a lot of myself energetically, I also love to give gifts. Most of the time, this fills me with joy, but sometimes I know I'm gifting to be seen as generous and therefore likeable. My manager Sarah will often catch me online shopping, raise an eyebrow, and say, 'Who are you buying this for?' She knows what I'm up to. Gifting is a love language and one you might, like me, speak rather too fluently. The five love languages are: words of affirmation (expressing your love in words and positive affirmation and wanting the same back); quality time (wanting and displaying full attentive presence with the people you love); physical touch (aside from sex, it's a touch of the arm, a cuddle, a massage at the end of the day); acts of service (small, helpful actions that make a difference to the other person's life, such as putting their phone on to charge) and receiving (and giving) gifts (not necessarily big or expensive ones; it's about the effort, thought and intention behind them). This framework was devised by Dr Gary Chapman, who is a marriage counsellor, but it works in and outside of romantic relationships. Dr Chapman explains how

I GIVE YOU EVERYTHING?

most of us enjoy using all five love languages in life, but we all find ourselves with one dominating language. Mine is clearly receiving gifts, which doesn't mean I just feel loved when someone gives me a gift, but that I predominantly show people I love them by buying them stuff.

This all seems rather harmless. You buy a gift, the recipient feels loved. Delightful. Ah, if only it were that simple, eh? The flipside is when either the gift is not received with the desired gratitude or you don't receive a gift from someone and feel resentful. Often, we hide our resentment in these moments and won't say how upset we feel. The issue here is that we can assume that everyone speaks our love language, but they don't. Their love language might be physical touch or words of affirmation. They might bloody hate shopping. But there is a discord created when you don't feel you're receiving love in the language you best understand. So if your love language is gift giving, carry on shopping, my lovelies – just be aware of why you're gifting and what you're expecting on the other side.

Never has my love language been put more to the test than within the framework of step-parenting. Entering the world of a blended family really ramped up my desire to please and be liked. I didn't have my own children at the time, but inherently understood that there was no guarantee I would be liked or accepted in the unconditional fashion that a biological parent might be. It felt visceral. There was instantly a deep understanding that I would have to earn the right to be in these children's lives, and to have their closeness and respect. I was twenty-nine, inexperienced and slightly out of my depth. Did I approach this delicate situation with care, ease and breeziness? God no. I ran straight into it with desperation dripping from me. My intentions were benevolent. I wanted things to work out, for these young kids to feel safe and tethered, but as always, I was in a rush. I'm extremely impatient at the best of times.

Being a step-parent is tricky and helpful mainstream resources for people entering a blended family have only really become available in the last few years. I was winging it every step of the way, often with my credit card held out, offering to buy them whatever they wanted. I must add that my step-children (now adults) are the least demanding, most respectful and gorgeous humans out there. Outside of the usual kid requests for the odd ice cream or cinema ticket, they didn't ask for much at all. But there I was, desperately trying to buy their love. What I didn't realise is their child brains wouldn't make the connection I had with gift-buying. They would be grateful and happy directly after, but the long-lasting bond I was hoping to create needed a lot more care, attention and time. I learned this down the line, and now know that spending quality time with them, listening to them talk about their lives and checking in with them regularly is the foundation of the connection I was longing for.

Time is perhaps the most precious commodity we have, yet we throw it away carelessly, often to remain likeable – which

I GIVE YOU EVERYTHING?

is ironic, as that is all time we could be investing in the people we truly love and in the reciprocal relationships that make us feel good. Instead, we say yes to things we don't want to go to, solely to mitigate the risk of being momentarily unlikeable. We put ourselves forward for tasks that will drain our time and actually bring little reward or benefit to others. Maybe we stay up all night making an elaborate birthday cake for a friend who would have much preferred us to get some sleep and stick a candle in a Sainsbury's cupcake. But somehow we believe that we have to show how much effort we have made to prove we are likeable.

One way to claw back small moments of time for yourself is to get off your phone. I'm not telling you anything you don't already know, and I need to hear it as much as you probably do. I may moan that I'm overwhelmed and don't have a second to breathe, but is that true? Did I just spend fifteen minutes scrolling on Instagram, imbibing everything from a video showing how you can make a miniature corn on the cob to Suki Waterhouse in a nice coat I now quite want to buy? Yup, yes, I did. Could I have sat deep breathing in my silent kitchen instead to try and feel a much-needed sense of quiet and calm? Yes, yes, I could have. Some of the time, we are mindlessly scrolling. It's just a habit. Yet there may be other times we are subconsciously searching for something in the metaverse. We want to find others like ourselves to feel a sense of belonging. We want other people to like our posts so we feel loved. We want to judge other people so that we momentarily feel righteous and better than them. We give so much of our time to content that isn't aiding us in life at all. I have to give myself rules like a toddler so I don't spiral down a social media rabbit hole. During the writing of this book, I've been strict about when I allow myself small breaks to scroll: the cut-off is five minutes before I must start typing again. I'll watch some AI fruit eating itself (why are these videos so addictive?), or online window shop, then get myself off social media before I lose hours.

But let's stick with this idea of giving ourselves away for a moment. This is a little different, a little harder to pin down, than giving our time, our energy or our emotional bandwidth to others. My job is weird in the sense that to present and communicate with an audience, you have to give over certain parts of yourself. This is a beautiful thing, yet can often be painful if boundaries aren't in place. During episodes of my *Happy Place Podcast*, I want to ensure I am giving and generous when it comes to storytelling. I cannot expect my guests to be honest if I'm not. I cannot expect my audience to feel in safe hands when I'm hiding things from them. During these interviews, I feel in control by knowing what I'm comfortable sharing. Yet when it comes to other people (namely journalists) interviewing me, I feel a lot less comfortable. When you have created something you want people to know about so they can find it, you need to do these interviews. At times, I've been unsure as to how much is too much to share, or I've felt pressure to answer a question I don't want to. As a people

I GIVE YOU EVERYTHING?

pleaser, I have said too much in the past and regretted it deeply. I've felt caught out, put on the spot and not strong enough to insist I won't talk further about a topic.

One particularly horrendous moment springs to mind from my early twenties. I was being interviewed by a well-known newspaper journalist who veered off into asking me about sex. He asked me what my kinks were, or something along those lines. I froze. As a young woman, being quizzed by a very confident and powerful older man about a subject I was deeply uncomfortable discussing made the floor spin. I stared at the multicoloured rug in front of me. We were in a suite in a hotel, alone. I didn't feel unsafe, just utterly bamboozled. *Would not answering make me boring, unappealing?* I wondered. He then added that a famous young musician, who was about my age, had said that wearing shoes in the bedroom was her thing. *Oh God*, I thought. *I know her, she is cool and smart and she seemingly confidently gave an answer.* I mean, she could have very well felt the same level of intimidation that I did. But it prompted me to make something up. I can't remember exactly what I said as I've mentally filed the full HD memory as HORRENDOUS, BIN IMMEDIATELY. But I know I felt embarrassed, unsophisticated and terrified about it being printed.

When I look back on this memory, I feel cross at myself for giving more of myself away than I wanted to. I felt scared and ill-equipped to deal with such questioning, but answered anyway because I didn't want to come across as uptight and unlikeable. But I also feel deeply sorry for my younger self. Although today's journalism is far from perfect, I'm not sure an older male journalist with considerable power would be left alone in a hotel room with a young female these days. Or, at least, I hope not.

If I could go back in time, I would tell the journalist that my bedroom kink was a neatly tucked-in fitted sheet, then tell him to go fuck himself. Anyway, we all have regrets.

So how do we keep something back for ourselves? How can we learn to say no and better guard our time so we spend it in a way that fulfils us? How can we salvage parts of ourselves and lock them in a box just for us? Not just emergency reserves, but enough to feel vibrant and vital. I'm in an interesting era of my life where I'm starting to really understand boundaries and radical rest. I'm on a constant learning curve, with plenty of opportunities to put rest and the art of saying no into practice. Recently, some very challenging experiences from the past were reignited. I got triggered and old anxiety and OCD started to rise to the surface again. Rather than keep busy and actively people pleasing by saying yes to everything, I chose rest. It felt revolutionary. I had nothing left to give, so radical rest was needed. My children went to their dad's home for the weekend, I cancelled plans I had been too worried to previously cancel, even though I knew I was close to burn out, and I did nothing. I let my body process the feelings I had been suppressing and allowed myself to feel

I GIVE YOU EVERYTHING?

the full force of exhaustion I had been ignoring. The world didn't stop turning because I stopped for two days. My mates didn't hate me for cancelling. (They all sent lovely messages urging me to rest.) And I didn't fall into self-loathing due to putting myself first. I'm pretty sure the more I practise saying no and hold back something for myself, the easier and more naturally it'll come.

What fills your cup back up when you have an empty tank? I'm not talking about anything fancy or extreme. It could be a bath. A walk whilst listening to good music. A massage. A very early night with a good book. Do you allow yourself the pleasure of it often enough? My guess is no. As I mentioned, my own reward system can sometimes still be too conditional. Do I deserve this treat? But when I do something for myself, it is surprising how allowing myself a small moment of magic changes so much. It's not only about giving ourselves a break from the relentlessness of life's constant needs and demands – these acts also prove to us that we do deserve downtime and pleasure. The more we do it, the more we believe it. We aren't and can't be just a giving machine, there to facilitate everyone else's wants and needs. We have them too.

Now I'm in my mid forties, I feel I'm naturally more aware of how much of myself to give away. If my energy is low, I care a little less if I'm not as perky in a meeting. Before, I believed I had to give 100% all of the time. Impossible. Our energy levels and ability to deal with everything life throws at us changes constantly, so therefore the outcome should too.

WILL YOU LIKE ME IF ...

I'm learning to let myself off the hook if I can't give everyone my everything when I'm shattered. I'm slightly less panicked that the people I'm around on those days will judge me for not being on my A game. Previously, I would lose sleep over interactions where I hadn't been 100% present and giving. Worrying that not making solid eye contact, or asking the right questions, would somehow lead to them thinking I'm a terrible human. My balance was off for years. I cared so much more about how I left others feeling than about how I felt. I would put on my best smile, be attentive to their needs, give them every bit of my energy, then go home exhausted.

I'm an introverted extrovert. An ambivert. I love human connection, crave deep chats, love physical touch, but desperately need to be on my own, like a little mole in its hole. I want quiet, stillness, no one asking me questions or even looking at me. Back in my twenties, I worried there might be something wrong with me enjoying my own company, but now I see it as an essential part of my personality. If I don't honour that authentic part of myself, I know I'll end up on my knees, exhausted. Other people exhaust me. Yes, I love a dinner with mates. Yes, I love interviewing people. Yes, I love being with my kids and family. But without breaks where I am on my own, I start to feel spun out and overwhelmed. Knowing our own limits and preferences rather than fitting into what we believe we should be is essential if we want to feel well.

There will of course be times you want to give and help. But when you know you're at burnout and have nothing to

I GIVE YOU EVERYTHING?

give, but feel a yes leaving your lips, stop and acknowledge if you actually have anything to give in the first place. Know that you deserve the right to keep something back for YOU. Protect your energy. Don't give it away as if there is an unlimited supply. It's such a bloody cliché but it is so for a reason: it's true. You can't pour from an empty cup. Don't be an empty cup that has 'resentment' in big red writing emblazoned on the front and 'yes, sure' on the back. Be a full cup that feels vital and energised, and is well versed in the word no.

Will You Like Me If ... I Erase My Past?

Slightly covering my face with my hands, I press play on my laptop. My own, much younger face is staring back at me. Chubbier cheeks, glossier hair. Then a looser, higher-pitched voice comes hurtling out of the speakers. In the video, I'm standing in Hyde Park opposite Amy Winehouse, who looks as charismatic and otherworldly as I remember. Diving into this archival snippet, I feel my muscles tighten. I'm holding my breath, I realise.

I have avoided watching any footage of myself prior to 2019. Looking back means seeing it, and I really don't want to. By 'it', I mean my past. Any of it. Instead of compartmentalising the good times, the euphoric highs and extraordinary opportunities I had in my twenties and thirties, I've almost deleted it all.

Seeing myself in my mid twenties makes me cringe. I'm blind to any of my redeeming qualities and only see a swell of naivety, a confidence unmarred by the trauma that's to come and a road ahead with huge challenges. It's too painful. Make it stop. But I keep watching. Half squirming, half fascinated. Who is this person? I feel so far removed from her.

I am very reluctantly watching this footage as one of my Happy Place team members has suggested that I revisit some of the interviews I've done over the years; nostalgic clips are very popular on TikTok. The late nineties and early noughties was a whole different world (thankfully – although, God, it does make you feel old) and it would be 'fun' to share some of these clips, was the suggestion. I recoiled at the thought. *But I've erased that version of myself. She's dead.* However, a couple of decades have passed, I am in my mid forties now and I have been in regular therapy for well over a year. I realise there is also a tinge of something else. Curiosity, perhaps? Why am I so scared to look back? Why have I turned on myself so aggressively?

So I watch the clip and then something strange happens. For the first time in years, I feel a deep compassion for little Fearne. In this moment, I realise I've run so far from her. I've been trying to get away from her for years, picking up the pace, covering my tracks with books written, serious interviews conducted. *If I keep pushing, improving myself as a person, surely, I can lose her*, I thought. Yet wherever I am, no matter how far I go, I know she's there.

I start to wonder how much of my running is due to my own propensity to want to grow and how much of it is driven by wanting other people to like me. If I can get shot of that ostensibly embarrassing, overeager and foolish iteration of myself, will I be respected, taken seriously and loved? But I can also see the similarities between me now and this old version of myself. We both just want to be liked.

Still feeling deeply uncomfortable, I press 'post' on Instagram and then hide my phone under a cushion. I don't want to look at the comments in case they confirm my fears about my former self.

I ERASE MY PAST?

I'm pretty sure many of you reading this will have tried to erase parts of yourself from the past that you find uncomfortable. Or perhaps you have felt the need to reinvent yourself entirely as a matter of survival. I'm not talking about a fun Madonna-esque reinvention where we dye our hair black and start wearing kimonos.

Maybe you were the insecure emo kid whose feelings were always too close to the surface, and now you are a career woman who wants to present a calm, capable front to clients and colleagues. Or perhaps you won prizes at gymnastics or athletics but you gave it up and now it's painful to think about how great you were at something you don't do anymore. Maybe you made a huge mistake, one that still reverberates through your life today, so you've condemned your younger self and see them as utterly stupid. That version of yourself feels far too scary to acknowledge, so you have covered them over with achievement or sensible decisions. A lot of us have experience of bullying, being picked on for an aspect of our young personalities that we then learned to hide as a result. If something difficult happened to us in our past, it can feel essential to forge forward in a way that ensures life looks completely different, to cover our tracks and not be constantly reminded of the pain.

Or maybe we're terrified we'll be found out by those around us. They'll work it out and then reject us. So we run from who we were, without looking back. I think a protective mechanism kicks in. We are so terrified that someone else will catch us out, reprimand us or want nothing to do with us that we reject our old selves first. If we do it, no one else can. We are in standby mode, waiting to be told we aren't good enough; if we bury those parts of ourselves that we know are imperfect and messy, we won't get caught out. We don't show others that we've been through tricky situations. We don't tell them we are scared. We don't admit that we feel insecure or jealous. We don't explain that we have weird thoughts in our heads. We bury it all, slap on a fake smile, put on our best frock, plaster makeup over the blemishes and tell everyone, *I'm fine*.

But what's the cost of erasing those parts of ourselves? Quite a lot, I think. We wave goodbye to the moments we tripped up and learned important lessons. We bury the parts of us that were brave enough to try. We say farewell to the bits of us that built resilience through hardship. And when we banish these parts of ourselves, we create tension. To suppress these undesirable parts means we have to put constant effort into attempting to keep them boxed up and packed away. It's tiring yet subtle enough for us not to notice the relentless attempt at hiding it all. We become used to shoving that version of ourselves down. We push and strain to keep a lid on it, yet it's still there.

I started out on TV aged sixteen with nothing but hope, the beginnings of a natural talent for talking and a huge lack of inhibitions. In my teens, I didn't care if others judged me or not. I didn't have the awareness to assume anyone would care

I ERASE MY PAST?

enough to judge me in the first place. I was simply me. How refreshing. How liberating. Wait, I want that bit back.

There was also a deep enthusiasm for literally everything. Everything seemed exciting and new, and my face would always show how desperately impressed I was. New people, new surroundings, new opportunities. I was so enamoured by it all. I remember being on set at *Top of the Pops*, feeling like I might implode with excitement, my arms twitching by my side, my mouth quivering in an anticipatory smile, yet looking longingly at the pop stars on stage who seemed utterly nonplussed about their surroundings. I remember wishing I felt like that: as if being on the *Top of the Pops* set was no big deal. Like being a pop star was extremely normal. I think I assumed their complacency must mean they fully deserved to be there. They believed this experience was their birthright. And I thought of my eagerness as demonstrating how lucky and undeserving I was. In my eyes, I was a competition winner lapping it all up and they were the golden chosen ones not impressed by any of it.

Envy led me to dull that side of myself until it was barely a flickering flame. I assumed that being unimpressed and cool would make me more likeable, less desperate. These days, it can feel like it takes a lot to impress me, and I think that's partly to do with this self-imposed banishment of that part of myself when I was young.

Of course, it wasn't just my desire to leave that wide-eyed, hopelessly enthusiastic young Fearne behind that made me want to run full tilt from my past. My late twenties and early thirties were a roller coaster of depression; the highs of childbirth; anxiety and panic attacks; and the joy of watching my little kids grow up. I would walk out the doors of the Radio 1 building and as soon as I'd passed the line of paparazzi that took my photos every morning, my smile would drop. It was fake, anyway. It would slip off my face like melting wax. I'd get in my car and close the door, sit back and let the back of my head touch the headrest. *I'm unhappy.* Admitting this to myself at the time felt terrifying but essential. I could only feel the edges of the darkness. Depression wasn't a word I'd applied to the sinking feeling until a dear friend booked me an appointment with a doctor. But it was there, along with the voices from strangers that haunted me, calling me shitty names, telling me I was terrible.

I don't like looking back at any of this. I would far rather tell you all the good stuff. And yes, there are loads of incredible life moments for me to reminisce about. Plenty to be happy about. But these trickier memories are the ones that have shaped who I am as a person. Yet deleting my past has always felt easier than dealing with parts of my story that I don't want to look at. Erase. Gone. Control-alt-delete. Let me start again. Please.

In an attempt to erase my past, I remade myself. I become Fearne Cotton Mark II. The one with a blank past. A robot with a clean slate, impressionable in all the ways those around me needed me to be. I decided I would strive to be smarter, well-read, articulate, knowledgeable, more serious, quieter, more reflective. At times, I truly believed I was exclusively doing this for me and for my own growth, but now, at the age of forty-four, I know a large part of this desire was driven by wanting others to like me. Around this time, I felt what I needed was respect, and maybe even remorse from the people who had me all wrong. I wanted to win over those who had torn me apart and publicly shamed me in newspapers. Only now can I see how much energy I wasted attempting to impress the wrong people.

I would meet people and decide that they were perfect: those who were pristine in their appearance, considered with their words, elegant with their movements, smart, naturally funny. These encounters seemed to reinforce the deep desire to erase my past too. *Surely, they haven't made mistakes. Surely, they've always been considered and smart in their every decision. Surely, they've no regrets at all.* I would quickly form a narrative where this person had lived a trauma-free life because they appeared good and perfect.

To stop myself from spiralling and self-loathing, I would then amplify the shiny parts of this new version of myself. Use longer words in sentences, pull my body up a little straighter, try harder to be cool and also to please. While frantically trying to forget my past – the heavy eyeliner, the cigarettes smoked, the bad decisions made, the clumsy words spoken, the lack of self-worth that allowed people to walk all over me, the bad haircuts. Delete. It's gone.

WILL YOU LIKE ME IF ...

The most dramatic attempt to erase my past occurred age thirty-one. As I lugged two large bin bags full of my old diaries from the boot of my car and dragged them across the driveway to my parents' house, I could already feel the weight lifting. Dad unencumbered me and swiftly deposited them into his garage. Tomorrow, he would take them to his workshop where he makes signs and burn them all in a nearby incinerator. In my mind's eye, I could see them ablaze. Pages of paper inked with my handwriting. Years of thoughts, troubles, stories and fantasies etched in my rushed scrawl. I had written a diary from the age of twelve or thirteen. I was fastidious about it. Every night before I closed my eyes, I would grab my little notepad and retell my day to my fictional audience in my diary. I was uninhibited. Free as a bird. The pen moving without worry or any sense of paranoia. I was writing for me. Excited by the day just gone. Dreaming big and telling all.

By my early thirties, all that had changed. I no longer wanted to document what had been going on. It was all too painful. I didn't want to remember, recount or wax lyrical about my days. I wanted to forget about them forever. The desperate need to start over was often the only motivation to get me out of bed. Becoming a different version of myself felt like a necessary evolution that would allow me to climb out of the dark hole I felt trapped in.

One way to keep afloat was to erase my past entirely. The diaries had to go. I didn't think twice. Mum and Dad looked

I ERASE MY PAST?

me in the eye as I handed them over, perhaps a knowing understanding tinged with a question mark. *Are you sure you want to do this?* I had never been more sure. Along with the parts of my life I wanted to forget, I was fully aware I would be saying goodbye to some beautiful memories, hilarious stories, and surreal moments my job had thrown into the mix. My teens and twenties were a chaotic bundle of years where days were threaded together with little sleep and so much adventure. There was no way my brain could retain every escapade, every celebrity met, every work highlight. I knew I would be losing a lot of it. But up it went. Flames blazing, blue and orange, wrapping themselves around each story. Goodbye, past.

It felt ritualistic and entirely necessary, and although I would love to recover some of those forgotten adventures, early days of romance and drunken nights, I don't regret it one bit. I know that at the time, it was my only option. Although I stick by my actions, today I understand that I have to find peace with the past that I can't actually erase. The diaries have gone, but my past hasn't gone anywhere.

Recently, I interviewed filmmaker Lorna Tucker and hearing her talk about her past changed my own beliefs about mine. Lorna grew up in a similar area of London to me, at exactly the same time. I may very well have passed her in the street as a teenager. Undoubtedly, we would have both been in cargo pants and a crop top. Lorna's book *Bare* tells the story of her homelessness, drug addiction and some extremely serious scrapes she got herself into. At times, I found the book so confronting. This could have been me. We are the same age and grew up ten minutes from each other. Only tiny moments of fate led us down our respective paths. Whilst reading the book, every time Lorna made a wrong turn, or trusted someone she shouldn't, or gave herself over to men, I nodded and thought, *Yup, I would have possibly done the same.* I didn't feel a shred of judgement. I felt empathy and a deep sense of connection to her story.

When we spoke over Zoom, I found I had hundreds of questions whirring around my head. I was completely in awe of how Lorna spoke about some heart-wrenching moments in her past. Injecting heroin, dating men who used and abused her, losing touch with everyone from back home. Hearing her tell these stories out loud only ramped up my empathy and gratitude that she has been so willing to share her story and speak about her recovery from such a challenging and treacherous past.

She is now a thriving, award-winning documentary filmmaker, but her new life chapter isn't about excluding this earlier version of herself. If anything, it seems to drive her. She lives alongside the ghosts of the past. Maybe not always comfortably, but knowing where she has come from, the hardships she has dealt with, and that so much resilience was built throughout it all. I didn't detect a millimetre of shame or embarrassment as she spoke. Her effortless storytelling

I ERASE MY PAST?

only made it clearer that Lorna has found peace with her past and isn't trying to hide it or make it more palatable for others. It's in book form, waiting to be read by anyone who wants to. She is telling her story not to be liked, but to give us all permission to remember that it's OK that we've fucked up, walked down the wrong path and done regrettable things. She is giving us permission to like ourselves regardless, and to care less if others don't.

Shutting my laptop post-interview, I felt a new sense of vigour. I pondered why I gave myself such a hard time, yet found it incredibly easy to feel empathy towards others. If I can sit and listen to Lorna's story feeling nothing but compassion, why can't I offer myself the same? If anything, I liked Lorna more for being so honest and unguarded when it came to the pain in her past. She has lived a life and is interesting and layered. Who doesn't want to be interesting? Living a life that's full of potholes and bumps makes you interesting. It gives you stories to tell, lessons to pass on and, crucially, strength. I find this so attractive in other people but have been failing to see it in my own backstory.

So how do we recover parts of our past or personality we have erased? It might not feel safe to do so if you've been ridiculed by others, or told you are wrong or not enough. If you were told in the past that your goofiness was annoying or your enthusiasm was too much, you may fear being disliked all over again. But what is the cost of losing these parts of yourself? For me, it was a feeling of being a little lost, turning up as a toned-down version of myself, which is draining, and feeling at times socially awkward and anxious.

I now know that it is far better to turn up as your full self. The one full of flaws, imperfections, stories, quirks and idiosyncrasies that make you *you*. We should be able to stand by those parts of ourselves without judging them, understanding that they are what make us uniquely who we are. If some don't like those parts of us, so be it. There'll be plenty of others that do. Those who love us for who we truly are. It needn't be a huge group, just one or two people who see you and get you. But I also know how hard this can be.

After I watched that first clip of myself from my twenties, I hovered somewhere between wanting to recover parts of myself that I had ditched but simultaneously not feeling entirely comfortable with the idea of embracing my past. I was scared. I still am, to a point. There are decisions I've made that I regret, things I don't want to look at, versions of myself that I really don't like. I was still under the illusion that if I only showed the world this new, improved, reinvented version of myself, then I would be safe. And yet that kind of illusion feels flimsy. There's margin for error and the propensity to get caught out. I can't truly erase my past, and I certainly can't pretend I wasn't an overly enthusiastic kids TV presenter – it lives forever on YouTube. You may see no problem with being overly enthusiastic. These idiosyncrasies that we deem unlikeable might be based on very little logic. To me, enthusiasm used to equal a lack of sophistication and natural cool.

I ERASE MY PAST?

Now, I see it as adorable and endearing. Somehow, I needed to get comfortable with my past.

In my late thirties my anxiety started to ramp up. I had been having panic attacks for a few years by this point and wanted to look for new solutions. I was tipped off by a friend who told me EMDR (eye movement desensitisation and reprocessing) therapy had helped her hugely. I did six months of bi-weekly EMDR therapy, which has an element of exposure therapy thrown in the mix. If you're unfamiliar with exposure therapy, it really just does what it says on the can. If there is something you really don't want to look at, something you are suppressing and hiding from, the theory is that the more you engage with it, the less scary it becomes. In EMDR, with the guidance of a therapist, you are gradually led back to your most dreaded moments, or the events or time period that instigated the poor mental health thereafter. You are encouraged to speak these moments aloud whilst either moving your eyes from left to right, or by using bilateral tapping on your arms. By revisiting these memories safely, you create new neural pathways that enable you to cope with the past.

Not only did I have some pretty gruesome moments to revisit, but also some versions of myself I had spent years hating. To put it mildly, I was not looking forward to any of it. There's no beating around the bush: revisiting it all was ghastly. But – and it's a big but – the more I mentally travelled back in time and spoke aloud these moments and the subsequent fears I have, the less heavily they sat in my gut. The less potent they felt in my mind. Each time I revisited, I felt something lifting.

Posting that archive clip on my Instagram feed felt like a form of exposure therapy. And watching more long-forgotten clips of me on YouTube was the same. The more I revisited that version of me, the less I disliked her. Younger Fearne really wasn't that bad at all. I had previously built up an image in my head of what she represented. I now think part of that image was based on other people's words rather than my own knowledge. I had perhaps conflated outside opinion with my own memories and created a mental caricature of myself.

I promise that if you have versions of yourself in the past, or moments in your past that haunt you, your memory and imagination will have warped and exaggerated it all. I guarantee that it's not anywhere near as bad as you are remembering. Nor is anyone judging you as much as you believe. They're all too busy judging themselves. I'm often reminded of the quote, 'Whatever you resist persists.' So simple, yet powerful. The more we try to suppress parts of ourselves or resist the truths of the past, the more potent it all becomes.

One of the Happy Place team members sent me an archive video of me interviewing James Blunt. I laughed out loud watching us drunkenly trying to push a car out of a mound of snow, then at a failed attempt by James to get me to climb

I ERASE MY PAST?

into a moving tumble dryer. Watching it, I realised I was less tense, more intrigued and genuinely envious of that version of myself for being so free. I nimbly bounce around the screen, all black eyeliner and swishing bob haircut. And I actually rather liked myself. I was funnier than I remembered. At times, quick and engaging. I was confident and uninhibited. I longingly stared at the screen, feeling a pang of jealousy.

Shit. How much had I sacrificed to mould into what others wanted me to be – or, more accurately, didn't want me to be? I wondered. I'd become so much more uptight, overly concerned with how I come across and perhaps too self-aware. I had filmed these silly, chaotic, funny interviews in an era before I started to get slammed by the press and bullied online. My sense of self was robust and almost untouchable. How the hell do I claw some of the good bits back?

A sadness set in that I had wasted years running from this perfectly fine young woman. I realised that I didn't need to erase my past at all. Of course, I was more naive, sometimes eager to impress, overly enthusiastic. I was young and inexperienced, but I had that glow of invincibility that twenty-somethings possess. Of course I made mistakes, walked down treacherous paths and did things I wouldn't today. Isn't that what being young is all about? Isn't that a defining characteristic of being a human being?

I had created somewhat of a monster version of myself that lived in the late 1990s and early 2000s. A monster-like, warped and exaggerated portrayal with swirls of black eye makeup and a grin that stretched across her whole face, with hand movements whirling as she speaks at speed. The more I refused to engage with that version of myself, the worse she became in my mind. Yet by ignoring her, I'd also forgotten her good bits. The fact that she was so enthusiastic and could talk her way into any situation. The innocence that made her see the good in everyone. The unfiltered approach to situations and conversations. The desire to try new things even when she felt out of her depth. I had been running so fast, trying to outsmart this version of myself for years, but had also erased so many parts of myself that I now missed.

I wanted that eagerness back. I wanted to meet new people and feel excited. I wanted to be wowed by someone's fancy house I was visiting, bowled over by meeting someone famous, euphoric at the thought of a new day with new opportunities. But how? How do I reverse some of the damage done?

When we bury parts of ourselves in an attempt to be more likeable, or to try to forget past pain, we are also piling on the expectation. Ignoring the previous mistakes made, or entire chunks of our life that feel too tricky to look at, means we are in danger of forgetting the lessons we learned and undermining the resilience we acquired. It means, in effect, we are hoping to never come up against anything tricky again. It's wild to think that bad decisions and big challenges only live in the past. We may be older, wiser and better equipped to deal with life now, but that doesn't mean we won't fuck up.

I ERASE MY PAST?

We will. But we can fix it. And we'll need all the tools at our disposal to do so, particularly those that were the hardest won.

The parts of my past I have struggled with the most are when I've made bad decisions. I see it as foolishness. Moments where I've acted without thought, trusted people I shouldn't or didn't have the self-respect to protect myself properly in certain situations. This foolishness has caused me pain, embarrassment and mortification, and has led to a dwindling self-confidence. But it's also given me some huge life hurdles to learn from. I've learned how *not* to do life. I've learned what *not* to say. I've learned who *not* to trust. Although I may internally believe my foolishness to be the most undesirable part of my personality and a bit of myself I need to hide if I want to be liked, I can also reframe it and see that in these moments, I was willing to try new things and act spontaneously – and I inherently trusted the world and people around me. These mistakes have also given me so much.

I remember a week not long ago that was rough. Two friends died out of the blue, which sent me spiralling, my kids were arguing nonstop, I felt like I was behind at work and ended up having a full-blown tantrum alone in my kitchen one morning after the school run. I nearly sent someone a shitty text, I spent too long on the phone moaning to mates about how everything was going wrong and I underperformed at work. Those seven days were not perfect, nor did I behave in a way I'm proud of. Yet I really hope the future version of me

WILL YOU LIKE ME IF ...

that will look back on this chaotic era of working full-time and solo parenting will do so with compassion and not try and erase it all. I hope she'll feel proud and know that I was doing my best with the time and tools available. Amongst the chaos, there have been moments of success, joy and resilience, so I hope those parts of me are remembered too. We are not here to get it all right and be perfect all the time. We are here to try, and try again, and to hopefully experience joy and love whilst doing it. Can you forgive yourself for past mistakes? Can you accept and embrace those past versions of yourself without judgement? Can you believe that others will understand you better if you bring all versions of yourself to the picture? Making peace with those parts of yourself will only bring you more peace and help you care a lot less if you are liked or not.

Will You Like Me If ... I Don't Age?

As I'm rushing out the door, I nearly forget my keys. I grab at them whilst finishing the short video I've filmed on my phone, I press send and post it to my Instagram feed. I race to work without giving it any further thought.

The video shows my face up close. My forty-two-year-old face with its slightly looser skin, thin lines trickling from the corners of my eyes, thicker lines like a knife has scarred a block of butter running from the edges of my nose to the corners of my mouth, and eyelids that don't sit quite as perkily as they used to. I point out each supposed defect. I explain why it's there. The laughter lines from the thousands of times I've been lucky enough to smile. The creases on my forehead that make it look like corrugated iron when I raise my eyebrows from the times I've been shocked, surprised or genuinely in awe. My cheeks, which once were two ripe peaches, now slightly hollowed out from passing years – time gone by that I've been privileged to live. In the video, I point to each line, groove and droop in the hope I can help normalise it. Perhaps it's a subconscious reply to the bombardment of videos I'm delivered daily by the algorithm, of face-tuned features and filters blurring out signs of a life lived.

I arrive at work forty-five minutes later, open up my phone and see that hundreds of people have already commented on the post. Many feel relieved. They've studied their own faces in the mirror obsessively, wondering if there is something *wrong* with them. Some are defensive, as they like filters, filler and face-tuning apps. Some feel keen to celebrate their own unique signs of ageing. It's noisy. I had no idea it would chime quite as much as it did, and I take ten minutes to read through as many comments as I can.

One thing is for sure: women are passionate when it comes to talking about ageing. The pressure to remain young has been around for centuries, but never has there been quite so much talk about it as in the last decade, with the evolution of social media, AI, lunchtime surgical tweaks and an all-round cultural celebration of youth. In the press, women are picked apart for looking a little weathered, having had facial surgery or fillers, and for simply not looking as they did when they were eighteen. Seemingly, whatever we do, it's wrong.

A survey conducted by aesthetic company Sinclair that includes the thoughts and opinions of over 10,000 women in urban and suburban areas globally states that 97 per cent of women feel judged for how they look. That's basically all women – half of the population – globally. We've been conditioned to believe that if we don't look a certain way, we won't be liked. We'll be unappealing, unattractive, unpopular, unvalued and unworthy. And when it comes to ageing, we believe we will slowly disappear, be disregarded and seen as over the hill. None of these opinions is based on biological fact.

I DON'T AGE?

They're rooted in a cultural story we've been told for many years. Women simply are not allowed to age.

My own relationship with ageing has perhaps been a little complicated by the job I do. For years, I was seen as a child; even after my eighteenth birthday had passed, I was talked to like a kid; the world of TV had infantilised me and needed me to stay childlike. I bought a flat and a car, had a long-term partner, two cats – and seemingly was still seen as a kid. Brands would send me tops with Hello Kitty emblazoned on the front. I was a young woman, but was told I wasn't old enough to host mainstream TV shows. I longed to age, to be seen as older and to be taken seriously as an adult. Weirdly, that way of thinking has kind of stuck, and I mainly view ageing as some sort of ascent to more wisdom and respect. But then, I'm not sure that's the full picture.

I'd be lying if I said the pressure to look young hasn't impacted me at all. If I spend too long poring over photos of influencers on Instagram, I know I'll stare pathetically at my less-than-perky tits in the mirror, wishing they looked like they did twenty years ago. I'll curse the relentless eye bags that sit grey and lacklustre under my lashes, and grimace when my crinkled tummy resembles a deflated balloon when I'm in a downward dog. As much as it can be a shock to look in the mirror when you feel twenty-two but have the face of a forty-something, I wonder how much of our scrutinising of our faces, our awareness of our changing bodies, is linked to how the outside world sees us? How much of the stress or pressure we feel comes from wanting others to approve of and like us? I'm imagining quite a lot.

I can happily sit on my sofa at home with my sloping tits, free, uninhibited and braless and feel just fine, but would I walk to the newsagent down the road like that? No, thank you very much. Would I panic about bumping into a neighbour who could clock my downward-facing nipples and judge? Yes. Equally, when I watch back some *Happy Place Podcast* episodes and can't concentrate on the audio because I'm obsessing over the bags under my eyes, I know I'm more worried about how others are viewing me. What will they think? Will they like me less and feel the need to tell me?

We are a society of women sucking in our tummies, crossing our legs just so, eyes flicking to our reflections in shop windows to quietly reprimand ourselves, arms wrapping around our waists, trying to hide ourselves from other people's eyes. The outside world constantly reminds us that we must remain juicy, sprightly, bouncy, peachy – like we were in our twenties. If we don't, it seems we have failed.

A quick glance at any gossip magazine or online showbiz news website and you'll see the contradictions thrown about freely, keeping women trapped and unhappy. One celebrity is shown in an unflattering photograph where lines streak her forehead and skin droops at the jowls. The picture has been chosen to emphasise that she has dared to age. The comments will come flying in. 'God, look at the state of her!', 'What's happened to her?', 'Bloody hell, she's let herself go.'

I DON'T AGE?

The next photo pinpoints facial tweakments or surgery another celebrity has had with comments below from readers who all have an opinion: 'Too much Botox', 'Oh, God, who's been at the filler?', 'What has she done to her face?' Mockery, judgement, slurs, all underpinning society's intolerance of women ageing or trying to halt ageing. We cannot win. Whether you age naturally or try to hinder its impact, you are judged, leaving women feeling as if they'll be unlikeable no matter what. As I hurtle through my forties and try to navigate a job in the public eye, I'm acutely aware that the older you get, the less relevant and visible you become. We culturally celebrate youth. It's constantly front and centre in the world of media. We want our pop stars perky, our movie stars cherublike, our celebrities youthful and exciting.

Without realising it at the time, I used to be exactly that. In my twenties, I was followed by paparazzi constantly, unable to understand what the interest was all about. They would take photos of me leaving work, out with men I was dating, catch me leaving bars. One photographer even booked and boarded a flight to LA to capture photos of me meeting my then-boyfriend in arrivals. At the time, I represented youth and excitement, so became perfect fodder for the constantly hungry media machine. These days, I am seldom followed by paparazzi. I rarely appear on the cover of newspapers and I am not talked about online in the same way. And although this is a massive relief and has hugely helped lift my general sense of paranoia and anxiety, there was initially a part of me

WILL YOU LIKE ME IF …

that felt less likeable as a result. As the years flew by and the furore around me subsided, I assumed I was not as popular. And whilst that might be true to an extent, I now understand it's got much more to do with our cultural obsession with age rather than correlating to how likeable I am. We want youth, and we want it now.

If, like me, you are somewhere over thirty, yet below sixty, you'll more than likely feel a sense of undeterminable limbo. You know that the outside world is not happy with you showing the signs of ageing, yet if you exhibit any younger attributes, you're mocked. You mustn't look old, but do dress your age. Dress appropriately, for God's sake. Put your legs away, you're not eighteen. What are you doing in a nightclub? Aren't you too old for that? You want to start a new career? At your age? You are not to age but must act your age at all times. Help, my brain is going to explode.

Luckily, I have some good examples of older women around me who refuse to age 'sensibly'. Meet Lin and Karen, my mum and aunty. My mum couldn't give a shit what other people think of her. She is outspoken, wears leather leggings and a three-inch wedged heel most days and loves to rebel and at times be outrageous. My aunty Karen is never without a large silver moon hanging from her neck and a fist full of huge silver rings. Often seen in a velvet cape, nose ring twinkling in the sunlight, she is growing old in her way. Neither of these women has decided they need to curb their own sense of style to blend in with the other seventy-somethings,

I DON'T AGE?

nor do they act in a way others may deem appropriate for their age.

Last week, Karen sent me a photo of her and my mum laughing hysterically, wrestling my dad to the floor at some sort of outdoor fair they were visiting. All I could see in the photo was a pile of humans, faux-fur coats, jewellery swinging, and wide, pink-lipstick-lined mouths howling. They do not give a shit.

When women do things differently, they are judged. At worst, they're shamed. How many older male rock stars or actors date or are married to women much younger than they are? We can all list tens of them and no one bats an eyelid. Yet when an older woman does the same, she is mocked and bullied online. Sam Taylor-Johnson has been happily married to Aaron Taylor-Johnson for over a decade with a twenty-three-year age gap. When the news broke that they were together, *everyone* batted an eyelid. A tsunami of gossip and negativity was thrown Sam's way in a manner that her male counterparts have not received. How dare she have a relationship with a younger man? The judgement was palpable.

There have always been different rules for women. Rules around how women should look, speak, act and age. Let's start in Ancient Greece, where there were assigned 'controllers of women'. That was an actual job title (there's a Greek word for it that I can't pronounce or type out here as I don't have an Ancient Greek keyboard). These male magistrates were assigned to ensure women dressed appropriately in order to keep the virtue of chastity alive and well, and could confiscate clothing if necessary. But this was a long time ago and we're nothing like the Ancient Greeks, right?! Well, in the late 1800s, it was decided that women couldn't show any skin in public, with necklines raised to below the chin and hemlines dropped to the ankle.

In the late nineteenth and early twentieth centuries, there were cases where women were arrested for wearing trousers in public in the UK. That's fun, isn't it? Imagine being handcuffed in the street because you dared to *cover* your legs (the irony).

Women's bodies have always been seen as dangerous. A tempting fruit that must be covered, concealed, kept away from prying eyes. But that sort of thinking has been imposed upon us by men. We have been indoctrinated to fear our own bodies. We might feel vulnerable having parts of our bodies on show, as we have been taught that isn't safe. And as we age, it's then seen as unsavoury, unnecessary and inappropriate. After caring for your own body for seventy-plus years, you're then encouraged to keep it well hidden in case it offends someone.

This is where we need to talk about the queen. Not our late queen, nor the Queen Consort, but our present one: Madonna. Another fearless woman ageing exactly how she wants to. Personally, I think she loves riling people on Instagram, with her raunchy photos of her semi-naked body,

I DON'T AGE?

clad only in tights, writhing around on a bed. Why can't we be and feel sexy later in life?

If anything, for women, sex gets better the older you get. You don't have to pretend to have an orgasm like we might have in our twenties to please the man. We can say, 'Nope, you've missed it, babe. Down a bit, more gently. Thank you. That's it.' And start to tell our partners what we want and close that orgasm gap that's still statistically bleak. For anyone wondering what that is, let me explain. Many studies, with slightly varying statistics, show that there is huge disparity in sexual satisfaction between men and women. This might come down to inadequate sex education, cultural norms, porn and a lack of focus on female anatomy and pleasure. With age, we know ourselves and our bodies better and can enjoy a much more fulfilling sex life, yet we are supposed to hide that side of ourselves. It doesn't add up.

I feel the most in tune with my body and what works for me sexually in my forties. In my teens and twenties, I was doing what I thought was wanted of me. It was so much less about my pleasure and so much more about pleasing the man I was with. I really hope it's different for the younger generations, but when I was growing up, there was very much a sense that we were taught to please the man in the bedroom. We were perhaps grateful to be seen as desirable (this could in fact be the sexual version of being likeable) and didn't feel we could speak up if we weren't appropriately pleasured during sex.

WILL YOU LIKE ME IF ...

The 2024 film *Baby Girl* was much talked about (and brilliant) because it challenged so many of these stereotypes. Nicole Kidman's character was much older than her love interest. She was a big boss, who enjoyed having her younger lover take charge, but it was always about her sense of pleasure and what she would be getting out of it. It was confronting and so interesting.

An older woman enjoying sex is still seen as an uncomfortable watch. We want our older women to be jolly, soft and smelling of baked goods. That's a wholesome, likeable older woman. So good on Madonna for keeping her sexual flame alive. Good on her for feeling sexy and showing us it's possible in your sixties.

A lot of the time, I believe women fear other women's judgement more than they do men's. Many women dress for other women. We want to be liked by females. As we age and perhaps tame our sexual expression, it's women's harsh words we fear. We don't want to be thought of as slutty or be taken less seriously by other women for showing some skin. We may find ourselves automatically viewing a middle-aged woman in a leather skirt with her cleavage on show as less serious than someone in a suit. Our eyes have been trained to see certain silhouettes as ones we can trust more than others. Ones we instantly like more than others. We perhaps fear other women's bodies because we are scared of showing our own, especially as we age.

I DON'T AGE?

See Carol Vorderman for details. Her IQ couldn't be higher. Her ability to calculate an algebraic equation is quicker than you can say 'Can I have a vowel, please?' Carol is more than impressive, and her quick-witted dexterity to solve any problem is second to none. *And* she likes to wear tight leather trousers with a big sexy belt and a boob-busting Lycra top. Many initially watched her on Instagram, wiggling her pert buttocks to camera whilst delivering a maths puzzle to the masses, and wondered how these two things could be true. Wait! What? She can be insanely smart and dress to exhibit her incredible body simultaneously? Yes, yes, she bloody well can. She can do whatever she likes. And so can we.

We can be a contradiction (which isn't really a contradiction, because it was made up by men) and dress in a way that might to some look incongruent and jarring. Carol couldn't give a toss if you like her less because she likes feeling sexy in her clothes. She doesn't mind if you concentrate more on how hot she is rather than being amazed by her maths proficiency. And she doesn't care if you feel threatened by how she looks. Again, we need to examine this centuries-old notion that we must remain the good girl. The one who has grown into a sweet, smock-wearing, toned-down, nice older lady who does as she is told. Looking back to the early days of *Countdown*, who knew that Carol Vorderman might just be the biggest rebel that we can all take a lesson from? We all need to be a little more Carol (whatever that means to you and your style – tight leather trousers are optional).

WILL YOU LIKE ME IF ...

Pamela Anderson has also become a beacon of light for middle-aged women wanting to rebel against society's norms. Just at the point where she was supposed to be covering the tracks of ageing and looking as glamorous as possible on the red carpet, she dared to turn up without makeup. I remember when these pictures first circulated online. My whole Instagram feed seemed to be littered with photos of Pammy and her bare face. Due to her lack of explanation (why should she have to give one?), nobody could quite work out what was going on. 'Is she unwell?' some asked. 'Did something go wrong that morning?' others queried. 'Had she had an allergic reaction before stepping on the red carpet?' another suggested. Nope. She just decided she didn't want to wear makeup that day. A middle-aged woman not wearing makeup out in public nearly caused the internet to crash. The level of shock excited me greatly.

As I've been raised by female rebels, I know that feeling well. Doing things your own way has been subliminally modelled to me throughout my life, so when I see a woman daring to stand out and go against the grain, I feel like doing a cartwheel. Pammy going makeup-free gave many of us permission to stop hating on our sunspots, picking holes in our supposed imperfections, and helped many of us to embrace our own unique faces. When she stepped out on the red carpet with her fresh face shining towards all of the glaring paparazzi, she wasn't doing it to be likeable, she was doing it for herself. Whatever personal reason catalysed Pamela's maverick move, we thank her for giving us all a little more room to do what authentically feels good rather than bending to societal norms. Pammy, you absolute queen, we salute you.

As well as bare faces, we need to see more bare older bodies. I'm encouraged by certain advertising campaigns of late that use older women to promote underwear. One brand, Understatement Underwear, has used an amazing range of midlife and older women to model their bras and pants, with loose skin, sunspots and veins showing. The photography is gorgeous and shows each woman looking so natural and beautifully them. This is what we need more of. Older women being valued, photographed, applauded, seen as utterly beautiful.

Our culture is not mirrored worldwide, thank God. Many parts of the world still hold older women in much higher regard. These women are called elders. They are the ones you turn to when you need advice and some wise words. Japan, China and South Korea all exhibit a deep respect for their elders. The values and wisdom of these women are revered and listened to, and age isn't seen as a slow transition to invisibility. In Japan, there is even a national holiday called Respect the Aged Day, which honours older citizens. In Western culture, we have wiped this role for older people off the map, especially when it comes to women. Older women are seen as less important than older men and younger women. Their life experience is disregarded as almost irrelevant. We do not put older women on a pedestal and say, 'Tell me everything you know.' We look at them with pity. And this is perhaps why so many of us fear ageing. We don't want to be irrelevant. We want our life stories to mean something and our lessons learned to be passed on.

I have a good friend, Donna Lancaster, who is, in her words, 'an elder in training'. She works in a therapeutic way with clients to offer her hard-earned wisdom, as well as her professional acumen. She is refusing to be less seen and heard as she approaches sixty and is on a mission to create more space for elders to be held in esteem. If you want a bloody good read, then check out her book *Wise Words for Women*. It's a gorgeous collection of thoughts and poems that will keep you on course to living an authentic life.

Here's the bit where things get complicated, because I am angry at some of this stuff, but still susceptible to all the ageing propaganda I see. It is powerful manipulation, designed to play on our insecurities, as I think we will all agree. I have one fist waving in the air, the other gripping tightly to a foundation stick trying to cover my sunspot. I was nervous to write this part of the book because you may well judge me. I also know that when I have to go on daytime TV to promote this very book, this is what they'll ask me about because we are all obsessed by this subject. *Bloody hell, I need to get my answers rehearsed and ready*, I always think. But wait – isn't the whole point of me spending close to a year writing this book to stop caring so much? So fuck it, here goes. This

I DON'T AGE?

year, I had Botox for the first time. I had it between my eyebrows, where there were two harsh eleven lines, and in my forehead, which was incredibly lined from having an expressive face. There, I said it.

After interviewing Olivia Attwood at the Happy Place Festival and stating to a huge tent of people that I had never had work done because I was scared, I internally asked myself if that was true. Turns out, I wasn't scared at all. I was boastful that I hadn't succumbed to the pressure we all face. I would stand tall amongst the Botoxed faces and show my lines proudly. But I didn't feel proud. I actually felt jealous. I wanted the lines on my forehead to stop taking over the show whenever I posted a video on Instagram. I wanted to look less angry when I wasn't angry at all, due to the lines in between my eyebrows. I wanted to feel better about how I looked.

This is the feminist dichotomy that comes with added complications thanks to the completely natural ageing process. We think we have to be one thing or the other to truly be a feminist. We believe we must forgo all care for what we look like because we are bucking against the patriarchy. We believe we must stand up to stereotypes and behave in an opposing way. Well, the thing is, I'm a feminist, but I also love nice shoes and lip gloss. I'm a feminist but I've been photographed in just my bra for magazines. I'm a feminist, but I don't want lines on my forehead.

Feminism surely isn't about bashing other women over the head because they've made a choice that works for them.

WILL YOU LIKE ME IF ...

Isn't it about giving women the freedom and choice to do as they choose without any judgement? So if you judge me because I tried Botox this year, so be it. I love looking in the mirror at my smooth forehead. That doesn't mean I don't think there is too much pressure on women to look a certain way (I've clearly been susceptible to that one). Nor does it mean I don't respect the ageing process and older women. Nor does it mean I will continue with Botox forever. Who knows how I'll feel next year, let alone when I'm in my sixties or seventies. I'm merely a very human, often flawed woman who is ageing in a way that currently feels right to me.

So, I encourage you to find your own way to age. Whether it's by dressing like a Pussycat Doll and dancing on tables, baking in an apron, dating a younger man, trying something new, going with your naturally grey hair or dyeing the shit out of it. The choice is yours. Age how you want to, whether it makes you likeable or not.

Will You Like Me If ... I Am Small?

I am forty-three years old. I throw my hands up in the air; my eyes are closed and my body is moving as if the beat of the music is pushing through my veins. The warm Ibiza evening air is wrapping itself around my skin, which is slick with sweat. I open my eyes as my face tilts towards the sky. It's the palest blue I've ever seen. The colour of forget-me-nots or one of those springtime butterflies. Internally, I say *thank you*. My grin is broad, my eyes smiling, my body vibrating with life. Lowering my gaze, I take in the beautiful chaos around me. Smoke pumped from a dry ice machine weaves its way between bodies glistening with sequins, feet stomping heartily on the heat-drenched floor, palms up to the stillness of the sky, teeth on show, hips swaying hypnotically. The clock has stopped ticking. I'm not worrying about what's going to happen next or what happened earlier that day. I'm present, 100 per cent living second to second.

For the first time in what could be months, maybe even years, my brain feels clear. The worry loops have ceased. The relentless thoughts have quietened. The stories I tell myself seem less relevant. I'm just here. With this new mental quietness, space seems to open up. There's now room for joy (without guilt), freedom (without fear it'll go) and gratitude (without self-loathing). I feel about as free as I ever have. Childlike and unburdened by the race of the day. I feel like I'm living big without any care for outside judgement.

WILL YOU LIKE ME IF ...

When was the last time I felt like this? I can't remember. Usually, my brain is cluttered with worries that stop me from enjoying myself. It's a low-level nervousness that keeps me trapped. If I enjoy myself too much, surely the rug will be pulled from under my feet. The wariness and general vigilance I usually feel is an eternal straitjacket that promises safety but actually just keeps me living small. My mind will often quietly whisper, *Don't have too much fun. Something terrible might happen.* Or, *You really don't deserve to be having this much fun. Think of all the mistakes you've made.*

At one point, as the DJ merges one song into the other and there are two seconds of uncertainty, I feel the edges of this fear. The anxiety rearing its head, trying to get attention. *Hey, don't forget about me. Listen to those fears. You're used to them. You know you're safe if you stick to the rules. Stay small.* Yet I'm able to shut the thoughts down almost immediately. I've never been capable of silencing them before. They've been too loud, too brutal to ignore. I don't want to listen to them anymore. They're boring. It feels terrifying but I choose to lean into the euphoria of the moment without panicking that there will be a consequence. I want to live big. I want my energy to fill the room, the flesh to reach the outlines of my clothes, my voice to fill the void, my feet to stomp loudly.

As my friend dances around me, spinning in her own whirlwind of sequins, mouth wide in a grin, I allow myself to take the risk. To do things differently. To dance freely and lean into joy without the worry that I'm undeserving

I AM SMALL?

or that something dreadful will occur. People I know, sort of know and don't really know at all come up to me, spin me around and stare into my eyes deeply. They say things like, 'You're back! I didn't know you liked to party? You seem like a different person.' For near to a decade, during the years my children were young, I rarely went out. And if I did, I certainly didn't let loose. I kept it quiet and small, and supposedly safe.

Until this moment, I'm not sure I was aware how much I had shrunk myself down. One friend opens up and says I used to seem so uptight and fraught. I feel gut punched but seen. Yes, yes. That's how I felt. I would try to gain control by pulling my limbs, thoughts and fears in close. I kept myself at home, my lifestyle regimented, neat, small. Maybe I was starting to break free from this straitjacket?

For women, living small means an all-encompassing shrinking. We want our men big and our women small. Physically small, obviously, but also not taking up too much space in other ways and definitely not drawing too much attention to the minimal space they do occupy. We must use our inside voices, not demand things, not think too much of ourselves – and never, ever be *too much* of anything. We should just obediently stay where we are put, like a small pot plant on a patio.

As we get older, there is a sense that we shrink to the point of invisibility if we aren't careful. The narrative that has been pushed on us explains that menopause, saggier skin, less perky boobs and a lack of fertility mean your work here is done. You are so small I can't even see you. You're supposed to fade into the crowd of other middle-aged women wearing Breton stripey tops and sensible shoes. Luckily, there are tons of brilliant women in midlife busting this shitty myth. See Davina McCall, in her high-heeled loafers and little white socks, for notes. Comedian Cally Beaton is another brilliant woman in her fifties who is taking great pleasure in refusing to age quietly. She wrote a whole book about it called *Namaste Motherf*ckers*. It's packed with stories and tips for thriving in midlife and living big.

It's reassuring in a sense that the cliché that you give fewer fucks as you age seems to hold true. Mates of mine in their sixties, seventies and eighties say they care so much less now about what other people think of them. But, as lovely as that is to know, I don't really want to wait until I'm eighty to live big. What about now, in my forties? Can we just sort it out now and not waste any more time?

If you are around the same age as me, you'll likely struggle with saying anything positive about yourself. Self-deprecation will come easily and compliments will be hard to take on board. I think Britishness has a part to play in this too. We are not culturally good at bigging ourselves up. We grew up in an era where parents told us not to be above our station and not to be a show-off. A time when magazines tore women apart for their life choices and bodies. The circle of shame

I AM SMALL?

was never far from a famous woman's cellulite or protruding tummy. We got very used to seeing women as inherently flawed, so we started to feel the same about ourselves. If the most beautiful, famous, successful women on the planet could be torn to shreds in an article, how could any of us feel safe?

We waste so much time worrying about our bodies being too big and therefore wrong. Muffin tops, saggy skin, big bellies must be hidden as they are wrong, we are told. Oh, but you can have big boobs, that's fine by the way. *What?* we cry, *I'm confused. So one body part can be big, but nothing else?* Yes, society screams back. It's simple. Boobs, oh – and lips. They can be big too. You can get surgery for that, you know. But you will probably be judged for having filler, so you're screwed either way. Big boobs and lips. But not your nose. (I'm fucked, then.) The nose must be cute, small and button-like. Like a Disney character. Got it? Then you'll be liked. Bums we're going to change our minds on, just to fuck with you a bit more. Far too many of us have wasted hours, years, worrying about the size of certain body parts. Or we have done many uncomfortable, unpleasant or painful things to attempt to morph and mould to fit ever-changing beauty standards. We try to keep small to be liked.

Having had bulimia for a decade in my twenties, I know how treacherous the conversation around women's bodies is. You can never really say the right thing. So I will talk about my experience and my experience only, which will differ from yours. I cannot speak for all women, as we have different body shapes, genes, eating habits, levels of body dysmorphia and so on. Saying that, I'm pretty sure that most women, no matter what age or background, have felt the pressure to keep their bodies small to avoid judgement at some point.

My likeability felt very enmeshed with what I looked like in my twenties. I was on TV every week, sometimes multiple times a week, and very aware of the eyes on me. A monitor was always nearby so I could check my hair and makeup on set, yet my eyes would never make it as far up as my face. I would instead scrutinise my body and worry that people watching at home would see my imperfections.

For women of my generation, not only did we encounter the media's cruel pulling apart of women's bodies, we also saw advertising that exclusively featured very thin women. This meant most of us longed for Kate Moss's tiny frame or Naomi Campbell's never-ending legs. In no way am I blaming these women. They just happen to naturally have that body shape. Good on them for parading their gorgeous selves down the catwalk, knowing their beauty and power. It is more about how our immature brains collated those images and that advertising. There was no countermovement in existence. Today's advertising may be a little more balanced, and the body positivity movement may be in swing, but we still have hundreds of years of conditioning to unpick. And for women who grew up in the nineties and early 2000s, we have to almost retrain our minds completely to know that it is OK to be the size we naturally are.

I AM SMALL?

I am quite small. Naturally, I have lean legs and long limbs, like my dad. But I also have the propensity to have a bloated tummy and very muscly thighs. These body parts plagued me when I was in my twenties. They felt wrong and too big. The constant exposure of being on TV made me hyperaware of outside judgement, so it became a near obsession to stay as small as possible. I wanted the audience to like me and I wanted to look like all the tiny pop stars that I interviewed. Falling into the early 2000s cliché habits, I went to the gym obsessively (haven't stepped in one since about 2014) and only ordered slimline tonic with my drinks, but I also developed an eating disorder.

I was twenty when I first started purging. I remember the first time as if it were yesterday. I had overeaten at a party my management was throwing. I have always used food as a comfort. If I feel stressed, out of control or tired, I eat. The buffet table had been packed with sandwiches, cakes, pizza slices dripping with cheese, gummy sweets and cakes. I hovered around the table and quelled my nerves with food.

Later, arriving back at my little cottage I lived in alone, I crouched on my bathroom floor feeling uncomfortable and disgusted with myself that I had no control over my eating. Instinctively, I went to the toilet and heaved up the contents of my stomach. It was too easy. I had found a way to rid myself of the self-disgust and the unwanted calories. If only I had known how unbelievably dangerous it was for my body and how worried my parents would become over time.

WILL YOU LIKE ME IF ...

I started to shrink. My body was closing in on itself. The smaller I got, the more I assumed the outside world would like me, but ironically the less I liked myself. I had a dirty secret and it was making me feel grim. The problem with body dysmorphia or eating disorders in general is that you're never satisfied. You are never small enough. The world around me continued to praise small women. Tiny waists, thin wispy arms, hip bones jutting, knees knocking together. Although the first few years were a constant battle of consuming food and then flushing it down the toilet, later on in my twenties, it became a much less frequent stress-buster I used when I felt I needed it. I still yearned to be small, but now ran on a treadmill and walked everywhere to burn off what I'd eaten.

We are constantly told that exercise will cure all of our problems and solve our mental health issues, and while that is totally valid advice, it's not for everyone. There is also a large number of people out there who don't know what a healthy amount of exercise is. These people, and the old me, need to be told that rest is essential. That our bodies need proper recuperation and stillness. Our tired bodies need hot baths, horizontal relaxation and time out. Some people use exercise as punishment. I certainly used to. I would push my body as far and hard as I could so it stayed tight and small and pleasing to others. I could have done with someone explaining that I could do exercise that I enjoyed, which was also gentle and easier for my body to deal with.

I AM SMALL?

I managed to completely wave goodbye to bulimia at age thirty, as I knew I desperately wanted to conceive, but I hugely regret what I put my body through all in the name of remaining small. Although at the age of forty-four, I have done a lot of work to feel pretty comfy in my skin and not abuse my body, I, like most of you, have days where I feel gross, bloated and full of self-loathing. I don't want to leave the house in case others judge me. Sadly, our generation is so conditioned that it takes the sturdiest of minds to beat this mindset entirely.

Do you keep yourself small so you're more pleasing to the outside world? Have you ever punished your body or limited the pleasure you can get from eating delicious food? Do you self-loathe because you feel too big?

One way I crawled out of the hole of bulimia was to face my fear of food head-on. I was terrified of binging and so didn't cook often – food felt too tempting. But when I wanted to try to reset my relationship with food, I knew I had one option, and that was to start cooking regularly. To touch food, smell it, play around with it, experiment. Being an all-or-nothing person, I dived into beautiful cookbooks, and I baked, cooked, stirred, poured and created every type of cuisine I could. I became obsessed with the process and slowly started to recover. Facing the fear of food head-on allowed me to rediscover the pleasure in cooking and eating, and cooking remains one of my favourite ways to relax.

We have beautiful bodies. Each one of us. No matter what its capabilities, supposed flaws, scars, lumps and bumps

WILL YOU LIKE ME IF ...

– every body is beautiful. We've just not been told so. We've been encouraged to stay small for so long that we feel trapped in loops of dieting and punishment, because we never feel our bodies are quite right. It's time for us to be beautifully and naturally whatever shape or size makes us feel vibrant and energised. My dear friend Poorna Bell has been challenging these pressures for some time, and her book *Stronger* is all about women exhibiting big physical and mental strength. She lifts weights, will not be told how her body should look by the outside world and constantly challenges herself to feel as physically well and strong as possible.

When it comes to women's bodies, the unpicking of historical pressures is not easy. To be honest, I have no idea how we can get rid of these tropes completely and entirely. I think they even change how your brain is wired. Society still values small women and plasters them on magazines, billboards, catwalks, the TV.

Although I have come out the other side of an eating disorder and care a lot less whether my body size is likeable or not, I can still feel utterly confused by the whole subject. I've been shamed on social media for looking too thin. My knees and ankles have always been bony, even when I was pregnant with my first child, Rex (I ate a lot of junk food and put on two and a half stone). And I have been circled in magazines post-birth for having a wobbly tummy when clambering out of the sea in a bikini. You really can't win.

So although I don't have any solid answers, nor the space

I AM SMALL?

here to try to unpack where we are and how we might get to where we ought to be as a society, I would say once again that life is fucking short, so if you want the cake, eat it. If you don't want to live a stressful, hellish existence where you watch every morsel of food that goes into your mouth, then don't. Challenge those damaging, horrible views of women's bodies and ask: who made this stupid rule, anyway? And if being small is making you miserable, look for another path. One that leads you to self-acceptance and more physical and mental peace.

Young women today seem to be much better at celebrating themselves, so maybe we should be looking to them for guidance. This is, of course, a generalisation – each generation comes with the insecurities created by the world around them, but I'm deeply encouraged to see so many young women challenging these stereotypes. For example, Florence Given makes amazing online content where she talks about living deliciously. Her 'Get ready with me' videos show her dancing around her room, carefree, exclaiming to camera how gorgeous she thinks she looks. Again, some women my age may cringe or grimace that someone would be as bold as to say publicly that they look great, but that's because we were told we weren't allowed to do so.

How terribly sad that it's normal and acceptable to wang on about how dreadful we look, how shit our hair is on any given day and how out of shape we feel. No one bats an eyelid. Yet when a woman dares to say she feels great and thinks she looks great, we mock and condemn. When you break this down, *what the fuck* are we doing? Thank God young women like Florence are bucking the norm and living big. We can only look to these younger generations and be inspired.

Staying small physically or figuratively keeps us in the shadows. We assume that means out of harm's way. That's what the ego wants us to believe, anyway. That we are safe there, in the darkness where no one can see us. But in the shadows, we are full of self-limiting beliefs and blind to our own full potential.

We are so used to being told we should live small that we have no clue what we are actually capable of. American author and speaker Marianne Williamson says, 'Our deepest fear is not that we are inadequate. Our deepest fear is that we are powerful beyond measure.' The first time I read this, I had to mull it over to really get a sense of what it meant. I now feel it in my bones. If we really acknowledge how amazing we are, how much potential we have, how big we can make ourselves, then we have to make changes. We have to live as if we know how brilliant we are. We have to move through life knowing we deserve the best and will use our voices accordingly. And initially, that is scary. If you can look beyond the fear of outside judgement and picture yourself living big, what does that look like? Would it mean changing jobs? Putting your ideas out there? Wearing brighter clothes? Leaving your relationship? Enjoying food? Dancing wildly? Loosening the

I AM SMALL?

tight hold you have on your day-to-day life? Giving yourself a break? Are you actually scared of how big and brilliant you could be? Do you fear others will judge you for shining that bit brighter? If so, fuck 'em. If people judge you because you're showing how brilliant you are, then they are clearly living small themselves.

The fear of living big keeps us trapped and worried. We don't step outside of our comfort zone in case someone shoots us down. We don't shout about things we are passionate about in case we are too loud. When you're used to living small and feel safer hiding away, it can be very bloody scary to put yourself out there. But it's not impossible. Taking things slowly and stepping out incrementally is the way to do it. If you've not socialised in a long time – whether that's down to social anxiety that makes you worry you'll say something weird, be judged, or just feel uncomfortable – then going to a huge party straight off the bat is probably not the best option. Steady and slow is key so you don't freak yourself out. In time, you'll notice no one is judging you anywhere as much as you think and your brain will start to recognise that it is safe to live that bit bigger. Smaller isn't safer. It's a trap.

So how do we live big and care less? I'm still on a learning curve with this one. I'm getting much better at caring less, but on bad days I find myself still worrying about what people might be thinking about me. Luckily, my job constantly forces me out of my comfort zone. My comfort zone is home. I could hibernate for days without seeing other

WILL YOU LIKE ME IF …

humans outside of my little family. Staying in the familiar and quiet of home feels safer and more comfortable to me. My job forces me not only out of the house, but to also have tough conversations. My podcast covers big subjects, and sometimes bringing up these subject matters can feel awkward or scary. But I have never regretted stepping outside of my comfort zone. I may initially dread it or have some anxiety, but I'm always glad I've pushed myself to try something new or have a conversation that I was nervous about. When I feel myself shrinking again, I look to great women who live big. Can we talk about Davina again? I could actually write a whole chapter about her: 'Will You Like Me If … I Am a Bit More Like Davina?' The answer is yes.

Davina is someone who shines very brightly. She hugs like she might never see you again and grabs on to life's glimmers, big and small. Her enthusiasm is electrifying and changes the energy in a room. During the recording of our *Happy Place Podcast* episode, she told me that she knows that some people don't like that about her. They may turn the telly off. Say she is 'too much'. But she is at a point in her life where it bothers her very little. She could tone it down and dim her light, but at what cost? To change her natural disposition would mean moving through the world with a lack of authenticity, which would subsequently shrink her world. Why does it matter if people find her too much? Doesn't that say more about the person judging than it does her? I think so.

So often women are denounced as *too much* in the hope

I AM SMALL?

we will lessen ourselves in every which way. We are too loud, too full of ourselves, too irritating, too strong-willed, too big, too thin, too sexy, too strait-laced, too bossy, too demanding. Tootootootootootootoo. It's infuriating. Which *too much* labels have you been dealt and how much have they stuck with you?

I've been told I'm too bubbly, too complimentary to my radio guests, too annoying, too stupid. There are more, but these ones have been like arrows stuck deeply in my flesh for years. At one point, I listened to the outside opinions and, in an attempt to be more palatable, tried to be less of those things. I've played it cool with my interviewees. I've laughed less and tried to sound brooding. I've overthought every word that's come out of my mouth and have studied as many subjects as humanly possible to appear more educated. But this is all so dangerous. My self-image became very wrapped up in what other people thought of me, rather than what I knew to be true. Their *too much* might be just right for me, or someone else interacting with me. So I was making myself smaller and lesser to fit a mould that didn't really exist at all. As I turned down the dial on all these crucial elements of my personality, I reduced all the qualities that make me uniquely me. Not only could I feel myself getting smaller, but a numbness set in as I erased parts of myself so they weren't too much.

My wish for all women, of all ages, is that we fully embrace being too much. I'm now very up for being too much. Bring it the fuck on. I am now – at last – aware that I will never appease everyone, so I might as well lean into those parts of myself that are a little bit extra. Some days, I want to dress like a ten-year-old who has run through a rainbow-infested jumble sale and then jumped into a pile of glitter, having been doused in glue. That might be too much for you, but it's just right for me. Some days, I want to be loud and brash and utterly silly. That might be too much for you, but it's just right for me. Some days, I want to wax lyrical – about a song I've heard, a painting I've seen, a pair of shoes I want to marry – until I'm blue in the face. That might be too much for you, but it's just right for me.

I urge you to write a list of all the things you have been told are too much. In a column next to your list, write a riposte that challenges those depredations.

So on my own list, next to 'too enthusiastic', I would write 'excited for life'. Then next to 'too full of herself', I would write, 'has found self-confidence'. Rewrite the list and find your power. Or simply see if you can quietly, internally find peace, knowing you're not *too* anything. You are simply you, and that is just right. Once we find a level of peace with our natural inclinations, we can shine as brightly as we want without the worry that others will try and dampen it. And even if they do attempt to, we will have enough knowledge and self-respect in our arsenal to quietly challenge those opinions.

When I look at the generations of women who have come before, I can see how the systemic suppression of female

I AM SMALL?

magnificence has affected so many aspects of life. Historically, women haven't been given the opportunity to bring their skill sets, dynamism and experience to most workplaces, so remained underpaid and in lower-level jobs. For centuries, women had few examples of how they might break through these barriers. On my podcast, I interviewed Professor Brian Cox and told of my embarrassment that I could easily name multiple male scientists in history but could only name one renowned female scientist: Marie Curie. That's all I had. Yet my lack of examples was less to do with my ignorance and more to do with the fact that back then, young girls weren't given the same educational opportunities as men, with universities only accepting girls in the late nineteenth century. In this case, girls were actively kept oppressed and in the shadows. If I look at my grandmother's generation, women were often dissuaded from going to work, so their main focus was the home and family. I don't imagine my grandparents would have sat down to discuss which household duties would be divvied up, or who would do the school run. The assumption that a woman's primary responsibility and skill was nurturing and caring for her family and home overshadowed any possibility for women to thrive at work and climb to the top of the ladder.

There might be progress and more opportunity today, but attitudinally and statistically, there seems to be a long way to go. Female CEOs are still a relative rarity, particularly in sectors like finance and tech. Female-founded businesses are far less likely to get financial backing. In politics, female leaders only make up 7 per cent of global leaders (heads of state or government) according to reports and surveys from the United Nations and Oliver Wyman Forum. And so on. Women do not have anywhere near enough opportunity to lead and be big in the workplace. Even when they do manage it, there seem to be different rules in place.

A powerful woman who asks for what she wants may be seen as bossy or, at worst, a bitch. This attitude isn't thrown about exclusively by men, either. Women have been conditioned to see powerful females through a different lens than they do their male equivalents. An assertive male leader is seen as strong, efficient and reliable, whereas a female can be seen as a right old cow. Do women at the top need to be powerful *and* likeable? Is that what we are asking of them? Do they need to remain soft, familiar and nurturing so that they're liked as well as respected? That seems like a big, unnecessary ask to me. I'm also not insinuating that all male bosses are arseholes, or even overly domineering. I have had a lot of male bosses and many of them have employed sincere kindness and support alongside their authority.

There have been times at work where I have so desperately wanted to be blunt. To say the thing or ask for something in the most basic and to-the-point way, but my fear of being disliked has gotten in the way. I've apologised, added unnecessary qualifications and squirmed my way around the situation. Yet, when others have been blunt with me, I may initially be slightly perturbed (because I know deep down,

I AM SMALL?

I'm craving the same freedom to say what I mean) but usually land on respect. I understand that person with clarity and feel safe knowing their boundaries.

Often, we soften our language and minimise our needs because we want to be the good girl. Even in therapy, I hear myself giving multiple excuses for other people before I say my bit. Delivering a disclaimer so I hopefully don't sound like a bad person. My therapist will often say, 'And what would your inner bitch say without all the filtering and excuses for others?' And then I'm confronted with how I really feel, which is perhaps angry or resentful. Underneath justifying everyone else's behaviour and my fear of sounding like a terrible person are the real feelings that I need to take seriously.

When we minimise our own feelings and desires, we don't take ourselves seriously. Every time we say, 'Oh, no, honestly, I'm fine,' or 'I don't need anything,' or 'It's OK, I'm more than happy to do it myself,' when we are not, we are making ourselves and our feelings smaller and more insignificant, so they don't take up space. If we want to reach our full potential, we must take ourselves seriously. If we want to shine as brightly as possible at work, or anywhere, really, we cannot squash our needs down and pretend they don't exist. When we take ourselves and what we want seriously, we express ourselves more honestly as a result, and others take us and our feelings more seriously too. It's only then that we can begin to ditch the narrow lines drawn for the good girl and begin to live big and without the fear of judgement.

WILL YOU LIKE ME IF ...

Over the next few days, I'd like to challenge you to think big. If you sense yourself shrinking in certain situations because you feel scared you won't be liked, straighten up your spine, push your shoulders back and tell yourself you will not get smaller. You deserve to take up space and to feel freedom in simply being you. Check yourself when you think you're being too much. Question whether that is true or just something someone once said. Be as much as you want and need to be. And question what scares you about living big.

What if you were to try that thing you've always wanted to do, dance wildly without care, wear the dress you've been too nervous to be seen in, compliment a stranger on the street on their nice cardigan, aim for something better because you know you deserve it? What if you shone as brightly as possible without worrying whether others would be intimidated by you or would gossip about you?

The British are especially good at knocking people down. Our mainstream print media has made a whole genre out of it. They would have nothing to print in the showbiz column without picking faults and judging celebrities' every move. This has subsequently slipped into our everyday subconscious. Knocking others down has been normalised, which means we might find ourselves doing the same. When we mutter 'Who does she think she is?', we're undoubtedly giving ourselves the same limiting margins to live within. This mentally keeps us all small. If we feel the need to ridicule others, it'll only cap

I AM SMALL?

our own growth. Would you rather stay stuck and cynical or be free and authentic?

But do you know what? Get too big for those boots. You've outgrown them, dear. What does freedom mean to you? What does shining brightly look like to you? If it scares you, I have a feeling that's a very good sign. Go big, you beauty.

Will You Like Me If ... I Like Myself?

YES.

OK, I could just leave things there, but of course I won't. Let's call the previous page my Yoko Ono page. Back in 1966, her famous work of art *Ceiling Painting* was a ceiling panel that featured the word 'yes' printed in tiny letters. Gallery visitors had to climb a stepladder and then hold a magnifying glass up to the panel to see it. In the context of self-love, it feels like the answer to the question 'Will you like me if I like myself?' is also in minuscule writing and often hard to find. Nobody told us the answer was yes. It was written so small, on a ceiling so far from our eyes.

Most of us haven't been taught how to like ourselves – or the importance of it. Most of us have been encouraged to place our focus on making sure others around us are OK. As children, we are told we must be kind to others, share our toys, always say thank you. And as important as those life lessons are, I feel like we weren't also encouraged to treat ourselves with love and respect and to be kind to ourselves. In adulthood, we are told to placate those around us, help those in need and give what we can. And whilst these qualities are integral to having a happy, healthy, community-driven life, we don't treat ourselves in the same way. For my generation, it was not passed on by parents or carers, nor was it taught at school. It's not their fault. They weren't taught it either. No wonder we are often bloody dreadful at it.

As you will know from reading this book, I have been a

people pleaser for most of my life. I also have a Type A personality, which means I'm goal-orientated, ambitious and have a sense of urgency in most situations, so, consequently, I take people pleasing very seriously. I have been the Usain Bolt of people pleasers, running from person to person with gifts in hand and a willing smile, chucking 'yes' around like it's going out of fashion. Yet as much as I love to help people out where possible, I know I've not offered myself the same level of service. I've been too quick to run off to hear about someone else's issues that need attention and completely ignored my own. I've told others to rest and take time out, yet run myself into the ground with work. I've been so much more bothered about whether other people like me than considering whether I like myself.

It didn't cross my mind to like myself until I had a chat with Davina McCall in 2018 at our first-ever, and much smaller-scale, Happy Place Festival, which preceded our supersized ones. She relayed a story about how a therapist had told her to look in the mirror each day and say 'I like you', which would then hopefully progress to 'I love you'. For the first few weeks, she said she couldn't even look in the mirror, let alone say the words. That night, I looked in the bathroom mirror and tried to utter those very same words. I felt queasy and could barely hold eye contact with myself. It was beyond awkward. Why is it so awkward to look yourself in the eyes in the mirror? After this cringeworthy endeavour, I thought a lot about how I had travelled so far from liking myself.

I LIKE MYSELF?

As young children, although we are beginning to be socially conditioned to serve others and place our attention on pleasing those around us, we are mostly unaware that self-loathing is possible. We dance freely in the street without a care in the world, we shout when someone takes our lollipop away, we tantrum when we are not being attended to, we sing songs loudly because it feels good, we express excitement without caring if others will think we are likeable or not. Small children don't really experience embarrassment and worry in the way adults do, because self-loathing hasn't yet entered the scene. It's much the same with animals. My cat Simon often pounces on Frank, my younger, slightly less savvy cat, pins him to the ground and generally attacks him, then gets up and walks away without feeling any remorse or regret. Zero fucks given. He doesn't sink into self-loathing or think about that moment ever again. (Until next time. Poor Frank.) And although I'm not suggesting that it would be beneficial for any of us to go and pin our housemate or partner to the floor, we could learn a thing or two from Simon about caring less.

I believe that liking ourselves is the cornerstone of all good mental health. Without it, nothing sticks. You can be practising yoga daily, drinking green juice, leaving your crystals out in the moonlight, but it won't touch the sides if you don't like yourself. I don't believe many of us truly like ourselves. We're not even sure what it means or feels like. For some, it's not a consideration, and for others, it's a hopeless endeavour that's never quite concluded. Personally, I know the importance of liking myself, yet have varied success in making it stick.

For the most part, when we are hating on ourselves, we don't even notice that this is what we are doing. It's such a habitual thought process that we have no idea why we are losing confidence, finding social settings challenging or – if you're like me – trying a new haircut every two minutes (I truly used to believe a new haircut would magically change my personality).

But what does 'liking yourself' even mean? What a strangely nebulous and overused phrase that is thrown about with wild abandon, yet so rarely actualised. Although there is room for the term 'self-love' to mean something entirely different to every person, to me, it means inner peace. A mental stillness where you won't tolerate self-loathing thoughts entering the fray. The goal isn't to love every flaw or supposed imperfection, but instead to love yourself regardless of them. To me, it means not hating yourself. Not blaming yourself.

I've only just started really feeling it in the last year. That's not to say it's been a consistent twelve months of pure self-love. It's undulating, to say the least, but I have both an awareness of when it's lacking these days and proof that liking yourself makes life so much easier. Let me explain. Like you, I have been through challenging episodes of life. When I look back to my very big bad patch of mental health in my early thirties, I suffered so terribly and got swallowed by the feelings because I had very little self-compassion.

I LIKE MYSELF?

More recently, I have experienced new life challenges, and I have dealt with them better. Not because I'm a new, improved version of myself, but because I like myself a lot more. Liking myself has allowed me to move on from other people's disapproval with more haste. In the face of rejection and the knowledge that I'm disliked, I am able to feel the upset, then move on. Ten or so years ago, I would have drowned in it for months, maybe even years. Liking yourself enables you to see the bigger picture. Rather than feeling fully consumed by someone else's judgement, you can see it simply as someone's opinion. It's not necessarily fact, just passing thoughts in someone else's brain. As I said, initially, you might still feel hurt – but knowing you have your own back because you like yourself and have self-respect allows you to live alongside that temporary hurt. To me, that feels like peace.

But what if liking yourself feels totally out of reach? Well, perhaps before liking ourselves, we might need to forgive ourselves. This has been integral for me to get on the road to self-compassion. In the past, I had short-lived moments of liking myself, feeling good in my skin and allowing myself to enjoy the moment, only for a ghastly memory of one of my many past fuck-ups to rear its head. Pop! The bubble burst and I felt foolish for believing it was OK to like myself. When the ice is that thin, it's very hard to rely on simply liking yourself. Forgiveness is a must.

Many of us are incredibly hard on ourselves. We can put too much pressure on ourselves to move through the world without ever putting a foot wrong. We give ourselves no room for error and replay moments of regret on a loop in our heads. There's an epidemic of self-loathing because we haven't been told it's OK to let ourselves off the hook. We hold ourselves to ransom and end up in a never-ending cycle of internally beating ourselves up. My question is, what's the point? What are we hoping for when we do this? Do we believe that by punishing ourselves, we'll beat karma to it? That the internal self-flagellation will somehow ward off other moments of regret? That it will trick us into being better people? Sadly, none of that is true. The truth is we will continue to make mistakes, piss other people off, say something we shouldn't and get things incredibly wrong – because we are humans.

What do you need to forgive yourself for? What memory are you torturing yourself with? When our mental health is poor (and I say that with no judgement whatsoever, as I have had patches of incredibly poor mental health), these memories are disproportionate. It took a therapist explaining the warped view I had of some of my past mistakes for me to realise I had things very out of proportion. To me, my mistakes were gargantuan, life-defining and unforgivable. Mistakes that were made because I was somehow *wrong*, whereas others were not. I had inflated these missteps and given some of them much more meaning than necessary. My therapist helped me to see them for what they were: everyday human flaws. With a more accurate perspective, I can now begin to forgive myself. I find it very easy to forgive others.

I LIKE MYSELF?

I rarely hold other people to account for longer than necessary. Wasting energy on resenting others or feeling hatred towards someone is draining, and although I've done it over the years, I know it doesn't work. Yet forgiving myself feels so much harder.

A friend of mine was talking about some of his past actions that have caused other people pain. Although he has now forgiven himself and doesn't feel burdened by them, he gave me some great advice. He said that it's healthy to wear the guilt and shame for a bit, to feel accountable and to own your part in it. When you have truly done that, you can start to forgive yourself. I think this is a crucial piece of advice because sometimes the 'love yourself' messaging we take on board can feel like a nice way to bypass accountability. *I love myself, I forgive myself.* There we go. Done. Don't need to worry about that anymore. Yet my friend's advice keeps us somewhere in the middle. We take stock of what we might have gotten wrong, notice it, feel it, learn from it, then forgive ourselves and move on.

You may want to get a notepad out and write down some of your past mistakes and get curious about whether you've sized them appropriately. Have you made them much bigger than they need to be? Are you allowing yourself to feel the sting of regret and sorrow? If the answer to both questions is yes, then start to wonder if you can forgive yourself. If you're not sure you can forgive yourself yet, what do you think is stopping you? You don't need permission from the person you hurt, or for them to allow you forgiveness. You aren't in control of the timeline with that one. Someone might decide to hold a grudge for years. In the words of author and podcaster Mel Robbins, 'Let them.' This is about forgiving yourself. Remember, there's not a single person on the planet who hasn't messed up, hurt someone else or acted regrettably. Holding yourself to ransom for life will not benefit anyone. Not the other person/s and definitely not you.

The cost of not forgiving yourself is physical tension, increased anxiety, negatively impacted sleep and a lower self-esteem. If initially it feels too difficult to forgive yourself, keep coming back to the notes you've made or revisiting the idea of forgiveness and see if incrementally you feel a little less averse to the idea.

This is not an overnight fix. In the modern world, we love a quick fix and often feel frustrated when we aren't instantly gratified. To forgive yourself fully takes time and also a level of discipline, as you have to keep reminding yourself that it's safe to do so. You could even incorporate this into your daily life by writing a note to yourself every morning. Even if you don't believe you deserve forgiveness or think it's possible at first, you can fake it until your heart and brain catch up with the idea. Once we have forgiven ourselves, we can move on to liking ourselves.

British culture is incredibly intolerant of self-love. If we witness someone complimenting themselves or celebrating their wins, we often see it as arrogance. If someone in our

I LIKE MYSELF?

lives sets a boundary due to their own self-respect, we can often feel defensive. If you have self-respect, you'll naturally set boundaries well. You'll tell others no when needed, explain why you can't do something they've asked of you and remain silent when you know an argument is futile. These boundaries may well rile others, especially when they themselves do not have boundaries in place. Yet when you like yourself and know your own worth, you set boundaries regardless of whether you'll be liked or not. You do it because you know you deserve the peace, space and time.

I'm learning this one on the job. Recently, I told someone in my life who has few boundaries in place themselves that I didn't want to discuss something quite personal. Guess what? It didn't go down well at all. They huffed and puffed and then didn't talk to me for some time. I had to push against my old natural inclination to go back on my word and do as they wanted. It felt uncomfortable and unnatural. Was withholding information from them mean-spirited? Or was I protecting myself in a way that I now deem deserving? I didn't acquiesce and stood firm in my decision, but it wasn't easy. The boundary I created made me, or perhaps my actions, unlikeable to them for a short while, but that's all part of learning to like yourself.

When we truly like ourselves, have our own back and know our worth, we are way less impacted by others not liking us. It feels like a skill, something many of us have to learn and practise rather than can just naturally do without thinking. Each time we push through the discomfort of others being pissed off with us or not liking our response, we have an important opportunity to practise self-love in spite of outside opinion. Can you really have your own back when others don't? That is the ultimate test.

In the past, outside opinions made up almost the entirety of my self-worth. If everyone else seemed to think I was insufferable, then I went with that. If I was momentarily celebrated by others, I would feel temporarily like it was OK for me to do the same. But darting between opinions of others to gauge whether it was alright to like myself or not was a flimsy way to live. Self-love has to come exclusively from within. Think of it as a muscle that needs bulking up. You cannot expect biceps to appear without lifting weights. Similarly, we cannot expect self-love without committing to exercising it. How you do that is entirely up to you.

Maybe start by asking yourself what it is that you need. What makes you feel calmer, more grounded, safer, more confident? A lot of it might come down to allocating enough time and resources to things that make you feel more like you. More time alone to gather your thoughts and recharge, or more time with good friends who make you laugh and feel understood. Maybe it's about prioritising a hobby that relaxes or stimulates you. How can you consciously fill up your mental and emotional tank to give yourself the reserves to keep going and retain your sense of self in situations that threaten to drain you? All of these things help us to practise

I LIKE MYSELF?

self-worth. You're quite literally proving to yourself that you are worth it.

Or you could flip the question on its head and ask: what are you denying yourself? As women, we have been trained to deny ourselves constantly – of food, fun, rest, solitude, compliments, choice. We say, 'No, no. I don't need that. Nothing for me.' This is where we have to take action to rewrite our personal internal rule book, taking into account that it is more than OK to ask for what we want.

Because when we deny ourselves, we are saying, *I don't deserve better.* This can lead to a subconscious (or conscious) belief that we don't deserve love, kindness, pleasure or rest, or only the barest minimum of these things. This is how we sabotage any feelings of self-worth. We may even slip into destructive habits that demonstrate our self-loathing. For me, it was an eating disorder; for you, it might be drinking too much, eating food that makes you feel wretched, working to the point of burnout, spending time with people that make you feel dreadful. We get into these situations because we don't believe we deserve better. You do deserve better. When you start to realise that, it means you have to make changes. But as soon as you start tapping into that self-love, however small and fragile the seeds of it may be, breaking free from these cycles becomes so much easier. You'll wonder why you didn't do it years ago. With any eating disorder or form of addiction, you might well need proper professional support to break the cycle. Therapy has been invaluable in terms of mitigating relapse and moving forward in a direction where I like myself a hell of a lot more.

Learning to like ourselves, or more accurately remembering how to, is a bespoke endeavour. We'll each hopefully arrive at it, whether via age and experience, a life event that catalyses it and/or (more than likely) through practice. It may wax and wane depending on what we are going through, but if the willingness is there, the recognition that we deserve to feel good, we'll be OK. However we get there doesn't matter, we just have to be willing, and remind ourselves that, with regular practice, it's entirely possible.

When we are trying to stick to a new habit, we need an incentive, and to say *You'll feel better if you like yourself* doesn't seem quite substantial enough. It's true that you will have an increased sense of confidence, have far less conflict in your life (thanks to the clearer boundaries you've set), won't say yes when you mean no (which always leads to resentment), carry less tension in your body and treat your body with more respect and kindness. But that might still feel far-fetched and out of reach for you. What I can guarantee is that if we learn to like ourselves, it almost entirely wipes out the need to be LIKEABLE. It might not extinguish it entirely, it is human nature to want to be accepted, but it'll take the desperation out of it so we can make decisions that work for us. For me, taking the desperation out of the need to be liked feels like a healthy goal I can continue to work towards. It's simple, sturdy and sounds utterly delightful.

I LIKE MYSELF?

Here are the things it can't do. Liking yourself will not stop others from flipping out when you say no or make a decision that works for you but challenges them. But if you like yourself, you'll still stick by your decision. Liking yourself will not take away the discomfort of knowing someone is pissed off with you. But if you like yourself, you'll be able to navigate the discomfort without turning on yourself. Liking yourself will not make life easier. This is the real kicker, because at first, it'll make things that bit more challenging. When you begin to respect your own decisions, take your own emotions more seriously and set clear boundaries, you're going to piss people off. Those around you who are used to you always saying yes, keeping them happy and diminishing your own needs will not understand what is going on. Their confusion might mean cross words, moments of conflict or, at worst, losing people from your life. None of this is easy, yet in the long run, it'll mean more mental peace, less conflict and less tension in your body. I also believe that the people who truly love you will only love you more if you show up authentically.

When we like ourselves, we can show up whole. We won't hide parts of our personality or past because we fear it'll put others off. We won't feel scared to demonstrate our flaws, tell tales from the past, admit our weaknesses, and be as naturally goofy, enthusiastic, quiet or loud as we want. Showing up completely as yourself without filtering or hiding parts of yourself is not only hugely attractive to others but also contagious. By default, you give others permission to be themselves.

WILL YOU LIKE ME IF ...

Think back to the last time a friend told you something they had been worried about or admitted an insecurity. No doubt you comforted them, but perhaps you also admitted one of your own concerns or fears. It gives us permission to be vulnerable and let down our guard. Equally, when we see someone shining brightly and looking happy in their own skin, we naturally start to relax and feel safe to do the same.

Many of us are waiting for some mystical future version of ourselves, one that has repented all sins and is supposedly perfect, to show up so we can then like ourselves. As much as we may grow and learn and improve ourselves, there is no perfect saintly version of us in the future. We will continue to mess up, make the wrong decisions and at times be utter arseholes. The trick is to learn to embrace who we are despite our human fallibility. We need to stop believing we can't like ourselves until we are perfect.

Liking yourself also means you are not scared to hold your hands up and say, 'I don't know.' So often, we think we have to know everything. We feel embarrassed when we don't understand a subject or haven't heard of a book everyone is talking about. If we already feel insecure and unsure of ourselves, we may be tempted to lie and just nod along with everyone else. Now, in my mid forties, I'm more than happy to admit I don't know the answer to a question or don't understand what someone is asking of me. And that is great; it has allowed me to learn more and be curious about the world around me. Through much of my adult life, I have

I LIKE MYSELF?

had a disproportionate insecurity that tells me I'm not intelligent enough because I didn't go to university. In the past, it's led me to shrink in certain conversations, get defensive with other people or put myself down. I've feared that if I say I feel out of my depth or don't know what the other person is talking about, I'll be ridiculed and liked a lot less. I've actually discovered that honesty always leads to more respect in the long run. Admitting you don't understand doesn't make you unlikeable at all. If anything, it's the complete opposite.

Recently, I was listening to a podcast that had Danny Dyer on as a guest, and his level of honesty was beyond refreshing. When asked why he hadn't ever moved into the world of Shakespeare, he simply replied that he doesn't get it. The cadence, language and storylines have never appealed to him, and a lot of the time he hasn't understood the plays when watching them. What a relief. He didn't feel the need to lie or counter his statement by then boasting about his extensive work with Harold Pinter. He likes himself, so could afford to be honest, which makes him even more likeable.

So, shall we make a pact? If we know that we'll be judged no matter what – that no matter what we do, there'll always be someone who doesn't like us, that we will continue to fuck up and be perfectly imperfect until our days run out, and that hiding away parts of ourselves will only lead to sadness and resentment – why don't we promise to like ourselves no matter what? Rather than the famous phrase 'I think, therefore I am,' shall we aim for 'I like me, therefore I am'? I used to believe in the mantra 'I am likeable, therefore I am,' which quite frankly got me nowhere.

When we like ourselves, others subsequently like us more too, but the important part? The right people like us more. The ones who stick by us whether we are having a good day or not. The ones who see us fully – shadows, tears, mess-ups and all. The ones who will always have our backs and will pick us off the floor when we can't manage it ourselves, but will equally celebrate our wins with love and enthusiasm. They'll remind us how great we are with a single smile and give us the space to be fully ourselves no matter what mood we are in. We then realise we don't need to be likeable to all; we just need to show up as ourselves to the ones who really see us.

Will You Like Me If ... I End Things Here?

I stopped writing a novel at exactly the halfway point because I felt such a burning desire to write this book instead. Immediately, I was faced with the discomfort of others potentially being slightly pissed off with me. Would my manager roll her eyes knowing I've changed my mind again? Would the publishing house awaiting my second work of fiction see me as flaky and unreliable? Would this spontaneous decision make me entirely unlikeable? But the urge to delve into this subject matter was too big and all-consuming for me to ignore, so I went with it anyway. And I'm glad I did. It's helped me to investigate why I have been so obsessive about being liked by others, by strangers, by those who outright don't like me. It's allowed me to get to grips with the parts of myself I find unlikeable. The portions of myself I have kept concealed behind a big smile and the word 'yes' uttered far too frequently. And where I might not reach full inner peace with those bits of myself, I know there is room to find acceptance. I know that waiting for others to give me the green light and tell me that I'm OK, not a freak, doing alright, nailing it, not a terrible person will never quite be enough. Like a quick instant online purchase for a pair of shoes I do not need, I will have a short-lived moment of gratification, which will then be replaced once again by insecurity and worry down the line.

The only way for me, for you, to find acceptance with the bits of ourselves we deem unlikeable is to remember that we are humans and not perfect little robots getting it right all the time – and that we can still like ourselves despite those parts. Many of the lessons I've shared in this book have been hard-won. I've trudged through gritting my teeth in silence, doing things I regret, utterly ditching myself, self-loathing to the point of physical illness, and periods of poor mental health. Yet, in the most clichéd way, as the years fly by, an inner urgency has kicked in. One that reminds me that this life is all too precious to be living inauthentically. We can live to please those around us, to appease and placate to avoid drama, yet it'll always catch up with us. The avoidance of short-term discomfort usually leads to a much longer-lasting kind. One that seeps into all corners of life and creates resentment and unhappiness. This is your life, and you deserve to live it, not just survive it. There will continue to be ups and downs, joy and sorrow, people who like you and some who don't. There'll be times when you are the hero and times when you are the villain to others. But the least we can do is experience it all as our singular selves. Not as the person those around you want you to be or the person you think you should be. Do it all as you. Unique, delightful, brilliant you.

Acknowledgements

I will begin this section in the most un-British way. I'm going to thank myself. Ooof, that alone might make you squirm. It's not the done thing. Self-centred. Ungracious. It's also the whole point of this book. For you and me to have a bit more gratitude and respect for ourselves so we seek less outside validation. I'm not even saying it with complete confidence yet, but I'm giving it a go. I'm grateful that I ploughed on with this book in what was a challenging year of change. I juggled parenting and other work commitments and didn't give up, and I'm grateful for that.

Of course, that's not where it ends. I could thank myself all day long but without the support of those in my life and working life around me, this book would be a document on my laptop and massively lacking readers.

So, thank you to Ebury Publishing who have championed my non-fiction writing and instilled confidence in finding my voice. Huge thanks to Olivia, Céline, Kaitlin, Anna and Lucy. And Kishan Rajani for the gorgeous cover!

Liz Marvin, it's been so incredibly brilliant working with you on the edit for this book. Your guidance and advice was clear, crucial and made this a much better read.

ACKNOWLEDGEMENTS

Sometimes my brain farts out many random thoughts and feelings, so to have someone help me make sense of them was invaluable.

Briony Gowlett at YMU Literary. Your enthusiasm for my very spontaneous idea in that very first meeting reassured me that I hadn't gone mad. To hear about your personal thoughts around being liked and respected at work inspired sections of this book that give it so much more depth.

Anna Dixon at YMU, thank you for not freaking out when I suggested pausing on my half-written fiction to pivot to a brand new project. Your understanding and generosity in my wild switch-up gave me the necessary space to write a book I knew I needed to write.

Sarah White. I started writing this book while you were pregnant and now you're reading the book with baby Posie in arms, which feels so special. Let's teach a whole new generation of girls to care much less if they're liked or not. Your support always means the world to me.

Lana June, thank you for always keeping me on track with timelines and deadlines and for listening to me have the odd whinge on the phone when I'm spiralling and overwhelmed. You are quite literally a saint.

Lauren Clarke. You stepped in halfway through the writing of this book to cover Sarah's maternity leave and have been instrumental in making sure Happy Place is run efficiently and smoothly as if you'd been on the team for years. Thank you for your support and encouragement.

ACKNOWLEDGEMENTS

And now I will curtsey to Mark Bekhait at YMU who is one of the most phenomenal forces out there. You have climbed to the top because you're the best and have given so many other women in the industry inspiration to do the same. You dress as if you've stepped out of the pages of *Vogue* and always make me want to do better and reach for my full potential. Thank you for always cheering me on.

Thanks to my long-standing PR dream babe Simon Jones for helping me get the book out there. Your ideas in our initial meeting were so spot on. Your understanding of this book has been essential and I'm so grateful for all your help and backing as ever.

This might be the wankiest thing I've ever written, but thank you to my therapist. This book would simply not exist without you. You've helped me navigate some very tricky times, given me clarity and tools. Your wisdom has seeped into everything I do and hearing you say the word 'likeable' in one of our sessions catalysed this whole book. I'm eternally grateful.

Thank you Alex Bedoya and Donna Lancaster, two phenomenal women who have shown me how to cultivate self-compassion and understand myself on a whole new level this year. With women like you in the world, things can only get better.

Nadine thank you for helping me out with the kids when I couldn't make the school pick-ups. You have been an angel in my life this last year.

ACKNOWLEDGEMENTS

Thanks to Ella Richards. Your friendship means the world, and your help with the kids after school has been invaluable to me. I owe you.

Thanks to Rex and Honey, my amazing babies. Watching you grow and navigate life is teaching me so much every day. I want to learn and grow so I can be my best for you. Here's to so many more adventures.

Thank you E. You have changed my life, woken me up and made me so happy. I love you.